Trevor Beer's
DOWN MEMORY LANE

Trevor Beer's

DOWN MEMORY LANE

RURAL REMINISCENCES OF A DEVON COUNTRYMAN

HALSGROVE

Originally published by Halsgrove, 2007

British Library Cataloguing-in-Publication Data
A CIP record for this title is available from the British Library

ISBN 978 184114 691 1

HALSGROVE
Halsgrove House
Ryelands Industrial Estate
Bagley Road, Wellington, Somerset TA21 9PZ
Tel: 01823 653777   Fax: 01823 216796
email: sales@halsgrove.com
website: www.halsgrove.com

Printed in Great Britain by
The Cromwell Press Ltd, Wiltshire

Contents

PART THREE - THE TREE OF LIFE

Introduction

These are reminiscences of the author as boy and man in the countryside, a spanning of many years spent wandering fields, lanes, rivers and woods in the Westcountry, with a chapter set in Scotland.

Naturalist, nature writer, wildlife conservationist and artist Trevor Beer explores both the humorous and the serious side of his country years.

This is a book for all ages, about the 1940s to the present day, of times spent nature watching and all that goes with that joyous pursuit.

Trevor Beer's 'Nature Watch' column in the *Western Morning News*, the Westcountry's award-winning newspaper, is now in its fifteenth year of a six days per week series. A daily column much loved by its readers not only in the region but all over the UK.

Read the behind the scenes account of happenings over a half century of one man's love affair with wildlife and the countryside, a passion which has helped bring 'Nature Watching' to life.

Trevor born was born and still lives in North Devon.

1

Beginnings

My interest in wildlife and the countryside began at a very early age of five or six years young, partly from wanderings on Sunday walks with my parents and younger brother in the lanes, fields and woods peaceful, back then, roads around the market town of Barnstaple in Devon, where I was born.

In those days it was never even considered that youngsters of such tender years should not wander a bit as long as it was relatively near ones home. The house we lived in was smallish in a terrace on the edge of the countryside in what we always called Pilton 'village', a sort of rural extension to the town divided from it by the lovely River Yeo. Indeed Pilton still stands in its own way as a separate area and linked with the village of Bradiford more than it is with the town itself.

I was two when the Second World War began, my eventual memories of that terrible moment in history those of a primary school boy who could not understand why all the iron railings outside our row of houses were cut down and taken "to help make tanks", my parents said. We actually had tanks passing up over our steep road one hot summer, churning up the melting tarmac, leaving strange tracks we used to walk in on our way to school. I remember, too, Italian prisoners of war being led along the same roadway and my father saying they were going to work on farms, dark clad men, silent and not looking about as they went. My father was an agricultural engineer for a local firm and may have been making ploughs and even 'munitions' but we boys were not told much. He also joined the National Fire Service, going to all the fires in the area as well as working full time and often at weekends.

It was of course the time of rationing and of Mrs Barrow's

wonderfully smelling General Store in Priory Close, opposite where we lived, which always seemed piled with food, yet we could only have what the Ration Book coupons permitted. There was also 'Cocky' Robins Shop in Pilton Street and another grocery shop at the bottom by the name of Gist, which often had huge 'Tea Fish' in the windows along with other food, all loose and piled together back then.

We could always get potatoes so meals were basically those, tasted up with whatever rationing allowed, people swapping food coupons for clothes coupons and so on with local farmers helping those who helped them at harvest and other times of need, when extra hands on the land were very useful even though there were a few of the excellent, hard working Land Army girls on some.

I used to go out helping on a milk cart on Saturday mornings when I became old enough not to fall off the horse driven cart. George Huxtable would hold the reins or deal with one customer and I would dip the metal measuring jugs into the wonderfully tasting milk and pour it into the jugs brought out from the homes by housewives or their children. I would also go to the farm to make pig swill for George, a jolly, hearty man whose shouted instructions brooked no argument. My 'pay' was a mug of milk which in those times was a joy to me, stilling the hunger we sometimes felt though to be fair we probably ate healthier back then than many junk food addicts do today. Cooking was on a 'Bodley', a black metal oven and range with a fire that was lit every day, winter and summer or there'd be nothing cooked. Our house was the last in Pilton to have electricity; lighting in my early years being gas burners on hinged arms fixed to the mantle pieces, which gave off a strange greenish light. To see upstairs we had oil and 'tilly' lamps, or candles. No heat other than the range of course, so on freezing cold lino floors the trick was to see how long you could keep your feet off the floor when getting up, or going to bed. I was very fleet of foot!

During school holidays, at weekends, or some summer evenings I would also help at a small holding owned by a Mr May. My task would be to collect jam jars full of cabbage white caterpillars, thousands of them from long rows of cabbages, or to 'muck out' the livestock buildings and generally be of help. I would be given cream and delicious sweet tomatoes to take home and once when I was very ill with whooping cough Mr May gave my mother a chicken which in those days was the Christmas dinner fare and a once a year treat, unlike today. We also ate rabbits, wonderful stews and roasts made from these then abundant animals. Nothing tasted better.

I mention these days as it was thus I found myself surrounded by nature and wildlife, growing up with it, knowing about such things as cabbage whites, bats, birds and other creatures and where and how they lived from very early days, even to having a pet hare for almost three years though she was kept at Mr May's as I could not have her at home. She was my great joy and friend and would lie across my lap on summer evenings after school and sometimes stand on her hind legs and 'kiss' me, a magical animal indeed, now sadly declining in numbers.

Momentous occasions in my young life were things like being trusted to take a herd of cows from the farm to pasture a half a mile away along the road all on my own. I'd do this regularly yet now I wouldn't dare with all the traffic using that road.

Those were the days, too, of the famous Clovelly Herrings, when there was herring fishing off the North Devon coast. Each week a fellow would come along our road with a heavy, wide hand cart which he pushed all day by himself, laden with fish, calling aloud "Clovelly, errins, Clovelly errins". There was also the 'Rag and Bone' man with his cart, a real life Steptoe, collecting left offs and any old bric a brac. Tough characters all, they had to be as the hills of North Devon, the whole region, are very steep in places. I never did know if he actually collected bones as well as rags.

Looking back on those times, comparing them with today, there is an indefinable 'essence' that is missing today and I am glad I grew up to know, feel and taste it.

At ten years of age or thereabouts I met 'Poacher Jack'. He took me on numerous jaunts about the fields and lanes on his travels, using these walks to 'suss out' the lay of the land and what or who was where. The war had ended when I was eight, Jack coming home from Army Service, doing odd jobs around the farms and such.

At eleven I went to senior school, an all boys school, and there was Nobby Nielson, our science master who ran a school Field Club every week. I was hooked. For me if it was wild and in the countryside that was all I wanted to know, my dream world a reality and it was to be so to this very day.

2

Early Days

Sunny summers evening in the late 1940s and I was walking along a pavement beneath the high wall behind which was built a dairy and some cottages, Jefferies Dairy as I recall.

Across the road where many houses now stand were open fields and Billy Lee's stables and, beyond, even more open countryside with woods and lanes, my favourite haunts.

The tall man walking towards me slowed and I saw it was Mr S.... known as Jack to the locals and with children who went to school with my older brothers, or had done for they were left school now and in jobs.

A bicycle passed me and swerved across the empty road to come to a halt just between Mr S and myself and I realised our local policeman was stopping 'for a chat' with him. I believe he was named Brownscombe.

"Hullo Jack, been out round the farms again then?.... let's see what's in your sack there."

"Nort to do you any good" , I heard Mr S reply and I stopped against the wall as he opened the bundle he was carrying.

This was the first time I had ever seen a policeman at work other than during the war when they and wardens used to come around checking 'black-outs' after dark in the Pilton area and once when a huge plane crashed into the perimeter wall of the farm at Westaway, close to where we lived and crowds of people were helping themselves to bits of metal and the thick aeroplane glass as souvenirs. Many ornaments and glass rings were made from the debris.

Two rolled up sacks appeared from the sack Mr S was holding and all were empty. Mr S was grinning as the policeman asked him to turn out his pockets and all I could see was a knife and string and suchlike.

"Alright Jack, just doing my duty, wouldn't be the first time", the policeman paused and looked at me, "and where are you off then lad", he asked, making me jump a bit as I had never dreamed of being asked by a policeman where I was going.

"Out". I remember saying as if that explained all and Mr S was laughing and saying that he would see I got home alright and suddenly the policeman was cycling away up the hill and the incident was over.

Mr S grinned and asked me if I was off looking at bird's nests and things as usual. He said he had often seen me along the lanes or by the stream at Manning's Pit. I told him I'd never seen him there and he laughed and said that that was the idea. He must have seen my confusion for he suddenly smiled and said would I like to see a bird's nest with late young in it.

I said yes and so began the friendship that led me to seeing so much of the countryside I had only read about in books for I was an avid reader even at that young age and every rainy day found me buried in a book.

'Late young'... what were late young I wondered as we walked up the hill toward Maer Top and up steps to gravel Path, a sort of high footpath running parallel with the main road and with thick hedge banks, ideal nesting habitat for bird life, and still there by the way.

We came to a plank seat and Mr S sat down. Taking off his battered green trilby very carefully he showed me four brown eggs nestling within.

"That's what the copper was after boy", and he roared with laughter at what must have been my dumbstruck expression. He put the hat still with eggs inside the sack he carried and we resumed our walk along the shaded pathway, coming to a spot where the hawthorn hedge joined a stone wall and iron kissing gates.

He bade me climb onto the first bar of the gate, pointing out where I should look and there in a well hidden nest were three young blackbirds all richly brown and speckled, mouths agape as they saw me peering into their secret home.

"Listen" he said and held up his hand. I could hear the loud 'pink-pink-pink' call from the bushes beside us and he explained it was the scolding of the parent birds as they were alarmed at our being near the nest.

I wanted to look longer at the young but he said we must leave the birds to it, making me promise not to go back on my own, not to look again unless he was there. I was told about the blackbirds nesting here since April and that this was the third brood they had raised this year.

And so I was beginning to learn why 'late' young and that schoolboy curiosity, however innocent and appreciative, could cause eggs or young to be deserted because the parent birds might be frightened away.

We chatted about birds generally and I learned simple rules of ornithology such as the fact that generally speaking the larger the bird the longer its young remained in the nest before they could fly. I had known for a long time that certain male birds had different plumage than the females and that the bright colours of the males were part of the breeding season rituals. It was Mr S however, who taught me that the quieter colours of the females camouflaged them whilst incubating their eggs particularly in species where the males did less of the raising of the young than did the females.

And so I listened carefully to all he said as we wandered along Northfield Lane and through Huxtables Farm, now all houses, to Anchor Mills near the Bradiford Village and Pilton Hill.

" If you want to come looking at birds and things with me again you'll have to be quiet and do just what I tell ee or else you'll see nort" said Mr S and I readily agreed to meet him at Gravel Path again on Sunday afternoon.

Looking back on those days I suppose to a child a poacher was a sort of Robin Hood in modern guise. Certainly, whatever the ethics of it all, they were a very different breed than modern poachers who are mostly a mercenary crowd. All that Jack poached he took home for the table, for his family. Oddly enough I was never offered fish or fowl in the years we wandered together. Maybe it was a poachers' code, as someone only recently suggested to me, 'to the victor the spoils' and they kept what their very real skills brought them.

As Jack himself said to me more than once, the birds and beasts don't belong to anyone and at ten years of age that sort of reasoning seemed logical enough and, after all, I had a new door opened and someone to show me the countryside more closely than ever before.

I was shown my first partridges nest one sunny morning, on the south side of a hedge bank where Jack, he had insisted I call him Jack, explained how they nested in a position that the sun will shine on before it has been up very long. Partridges hate wind he said and it was a waste of time looking for their nests on the north or west sides of a bank or wood because of the prevailing wind.

"They'll choose the spot carefully and are very crafty at using a rise in the ground or a clump of gorse or brambles to hide" he said.

He showed me how in most cases the birds usually had a small branch of blackberry or some such arching over the nest, the leaves helping to screen the bird from the hot sun and also to hide her from sight.

Cats were the worst enemy to birds like partridges he told me, far worse than foxes for example and indeed one farm cat we knew very well in those days used to hunt the fields and hedges around Westaway and Trayne farms with great success and also put a fox or two to their heels.

Of course partridges are fewer than they used to be but in the frosty dusk of a March evening one can hear them calling, or watch them peck at newly sown ground in April and anyone who knows his ground well should be able to locate their nests in late May. Sites that are ideal are limited and a good naturalist does his homework in advance.

"That run going straight up the hedge, that'll be rabbit...", he told me "...but that tiny run further along will likely be partridge, see how it goes in sideways", he said.

I could make out the diagonal run of some creature disappearing under bramble and fern and said should we go and look.

"No, not now, in the morning..." he told me "...the female will likely be in there now and usually lays between nine and twelve o'clock so we wont come back this way until mid-afternoon, no need to upset her", he said.

It was in this way I learned the great patience of the man and learned to be patient myself. How it has stood me in good stead whilst wildlife watching over the years.

3

About Fish & Waterways

One afternoon I met Jack by the old mill near Derby at the edge of Barnstaple, known locally as Roth's Mill and close to where the old Lynton Railway used to run. I had been sitting on the iron rail fence of a little wooden footbridge watching trout slipping upstream when I heard a low whistle. Jack was there in the shadows of a hawthorn tree his khaki shirt and dark trousers rendering him almost invisible.

He motioned me to slow down as I began to run across the field and his voice was sharp and reproving as he told me to walk slow and quiet always. I never ran to him again.

"Come on then boy" and his grin was suddenly friendly as he walked away silently along the riverbank his eyes to the water.

After some minutes of fast walking we were some fields upstream when he suddenly put up his hand and stopped, pointing into the water. "Trout" he said quietly and dropped to his knees in the cover of sallow bushes waving to me to do the same. Fumbling in his khaki rucksack he pulled a knife from his pack and cut a slim ash stick from a tree growing next to a stand of sallow and elder.

"Use ash when you can, it is whippy and strong, light too", he said as he shredded the leaves off and tied a thin wire to the narrowest end telling me to remember it must be tied behind a notch where a leafy twig had been stripped off so that it would not slip.

Jack then made the noose in the copper wire, testing it to see it tightened and slipped loose easily.

"Never make the noose too big or the fish'll get out before you can get'n", he whispered and as he spoke he crept on all fours to the water edge, motioning me to lie beside him. I was afraid to breathe.

'"Keep still and don't let your shadow on the water boy".

I kept very still as Jack moved his rod out over the water and the thin wire slipped beneath the surface becoming part of the river. It touched the bottom and a tiny cloud of mud moved toward the fish. I could see its jaws moving.

Nearer the noose went and I found my mouth hurt where I had clamped my teeth together in excitement.

The sunlit water ripples hid the wire glints and then I saw the noose slide over the trout's head and gills and past the first fins until it was about a third of the way along the creature from its end. The fish did not move. I couldn't believe it. Nothing moved, I was paralysed and Jacks arm was rigid. Suddenly his arm and body jerked as one and I jumped as the large fish landed with a thump on the bank beside us and it was all over in seconds.

As Jack packed his gear and the fish into a paper bag brought from his rucksack he told me it was possible to catch a fish with just a loop made in an osier which he explained was a sort of willow found by the water.

"Don't even need a wire then, it all grows where you want it but the noose is harder to work in an osier" he said as we walked on along the bank. I walked and trotted to keep up with his stride through the high buttercups as he told me the names of the birds we saw and some of the butterflies.

He called the Wren a Crackie, the Blue Tit a Tom Tit and I always knew the birds by these names, and the moorhen by the name Dipchick.

This use of Dipchick as the common Devon name for moorhens still causes confusion today amongst visiting bird-watchers who know well from the books the Little Grebe or Dabchick.

I well recall the excitement of a number of these when informed how common dipchicks were hereabouts as a breed-ing species. Find them on every pond and stream in North Devon they'd be told and off they would go in search of the Little Grebes, which in fact do breed in North Devon but only rarely.

It was on another lovely summers day that we again went fishing during school summer holidays. We were along a secluded valley about a hundred paces above a weir, a place which is still good for trout and other fish and much loved by grey herons which Jack called 'Cranes.'

I asked if he was going to use the wire noose again and he said no, pointing to where he wanted me to sit. On this occasion his Jack Russell dog, Tim, was with us and he immediately moved to sit beside me where his master had pointed.

Jack rolled up his shirt sleeves and leaned out slightly over the water where a deep pool had been created by a sharp meander in the waterway.

Without any sign of a ripple his arm slid beneath the water, becoming strangely white and disjointed by the refraction as he leaned further in. From where I crouched I could not see the process but he later explained that he actually gently rubbed, or tickled, the belly of the fish and that this seemed to lull it enough for a sudden snatch to jerk it clear of the water. Some fish, he said, actually rose slowly towards the surface as they were tickled and this made the snatch that much easier.

On the couple of occasions I tried this method of fishing I found the water breathtakingly cold by the time ones shoulder was reached and once I actually lifted my feet, bent my legs up to reach deeper and slowly slid below the surface with a great yell. Needless to say I was in deep trouble and much hot water when I arrived home in a more dishevelled state than I could hide.

It was along these waterways that I first learned of otters in the days before mink had arrived in North Devon. We used to see them occasionally of an evening moving upstream alone or sometimes with cubs along the banks. Jack made little mention of them other than they ate fish and took a lot of eels and it was not until many years later that the otter suddenly became extremely rare in the British countryside, or at least it was suddenly noticed that this was the case.

Jack's dog Tim was a real character and when we were out all day Jack would carry enough food for us both to eat when the sun was highest and we would sit under trees. It was either bread and meat or cheese, or some kind of pasties, which were home made. He always fed some of what he had to Tim who would then go to the stream to drink and lie in the coolest spot in high grass. In fact wherever we walked the little terrier would use the shade. Often he would shove his head and shoulders down a rabbit hole and bark away, the sound muffled but rarely did the wiley rabbits emerge with him around.

I well recall one sharply cold October day Jack and I were along a valley stream when we saw two men at the waters edge under oak and alder trees. At this spot there is a small island with two trees and a largish pool just below it.

"It's the L.... brothers" Jack said naming one of the local families whose descendents are still wise in the ways of the river to this day. He motioned me to hide behind the hedge bank dividing the field we were in from the next in which were the two men, and Jack moved into hiding beside me.

Suddenly he raised himself slightly and shouted...

"There they both be boys, get round behind 'em!"

Peering over the hedge we saw the two men leave the waterside at a run and disappear into the adjoining lane. We could make out their heads bobbing as they ran up the slope, mostly hidden by the hazel hedges and then they were out of sight.

"They'll hide in the old quarry" Jack said and clapped me hard on the shoulder, a sign to stay where I was. I watched him hare across the field to where the men had been crouching, his long legs covering the ground at great speed.

He was soon back with two fine salmon wrapped in ferns.

"Got yer just right we did boy, they ad six beauties over there but four's enough for em when they gets back".

Salmon and sea trout were favourites of Jack and his family at this time of year, and sold well too at the back doors of local inns and hotels.

Often we would watch the spring and autumn runs of these magnificent fish as they leapt at the foaming weirs or lay quivering powerfully as they drove themselves up the steps of the fish passes, fighting their way over the black polished glassiness of the weir tops. Always one of these fish would not make it to the reeds if Jack was about.

The penetration of salmon and trout into the waterways of the Taw and Torridge and their tributaries is a remarkable sight. Those used to fishing the expensive beats are the real 'sporting' anglers pitting their skills against the great fish on waters swift or where pools swirl deeply neath steep grassy banks.

No less skilled are the poachers though their choice of beat is where they can better guarantee good catches by whatever means, be it by gaff, stake nets or whatever. I was shown one spot when I was eleven or so that is still used by small salmon, a waterway some thirty inches wide and about twenty inches deep for many yards under a wood.

My job then was to lie in wait, watching for the dark shapes to pass by my still head, then to drop a board neatly into place behind their tails. My doing this was the signal Jack would require to immediately move from the stream further up stream to do the same with a similar board.

It was then but a simple matter for Jack to catch two or three whereupon the boards and fish would be hidden and away we'd go.

On good days, that is when Jack had caught more than he wanted we would go home via a part of Barnstaple called Ladywell, passing Pilton Church to knock on the door of a little cottage built into the arch at the top of Pilton Street.

An old woman lived there, bent of shoulder and always slippered and bound with a huge housecoat. She never went further than the nearest shop and she would often wait on her doorstep for school to finish for the day and one or another of us youngsters would fetch her shopping.

Jack would knock on the blackened, ancient doorway under the arch and soon we would hear the huge key turn, the door opening just enough to allow her to see who was bothering her day.

"Bessie, there'll be a fish for ee' about eight tonight so answer the door maid won't ee".

"Ah, you'm a good boy Jack, do ee want a cuppa tay?"

Sometimes we would stay for a cup in the shining little front room with its diamond shaped leaded lights overlooking the steep hill of Pilton.

I used to watch passers by as she and Jack chatted, or gaze wonderingly at the kingfisher under its glass dome on the sideboard. Even though the bird was familiar to me in the wild to see one so close in all its fine detail always fascinated me.

Bessie was not a relative of Jacks but he knew everyone in the area one way or another and she was obviously 'special' and someone he felt could do with a bit of help occasionally. It was not until years later that I discovered she was related to my mother who called her Aunt Bessie.

Ladywell itself is a grouping of cottages near the church and reached via narrow lanes, 'quaint' tourists would call it today I suppose, though it is not a term I like. The lane from the cottages to Pilton runs under a huge brick building which was then a thriving glove factory, and on the other side are high walls forming part of the school and church buildings.

Jack knew many of the glove workers and often we would pause at the windows, looking down into the deep well of the factory rooms to attract their attention.

On one of these days Jack was chatting to a workman putting out huge cardboard boxes against the lane wall we noticed one of the Ladywell residents peering round the corner from his home and obviously listening.

"Old R.. has got 'is nose in other people's business at usual Jack", grinned his friend Tom.

"Aye, what can us do 'bout it Tom, little bit of fun like?"

"Tell ee what Jack, you play along with me" Tom said quietly and then out loud...

"Ow about getting me a pheasant or two then Jack, long time since me and the missus ad a good pheasant?".

"No trouble Tom, got me eye on some for tonight if ee likes".

"Tonight's perfect matey, put 'em in this top box and I'll be round for 'em about nine o'clock tonight when tis dark".

Tom went back inside the factory and we wandered off along the lane, turning right at the end of the walk down the little hill leading to the main road. Tom was waiting for us at another door with a huge grin on his face.

"Lovely Jack, old R... will get there well before nine if I knows him".

"De ee think ee'll split on us then Tom and 'ope at ave us caught?"

"Oh no, ee'll be after the pheasant sure enough, knowin we can't say nort about it, but I tell what I got in mind".

And Tom outlined his 'bit of fun' for that evening, a plan of great schoolboy prankishness such as stays within many an adult male however they may age.

That night I got permission to be out at a friends until nine or so and met Jack at Tom's house which was not far from the factory, at sixish. We drank tea and listened to the wireless until eight. Tom's wife, a pleasant woman, was in on the plan and kept chuckling and saying 'you'll never grow up Tom but I'd love to see old Rs face".

Old R... had a reputation for nosiness and for passing tales and gossip around. A 'mean streak' Tom called it. He would even call at our school to tell the head when he saw any of us playing football in the road and that sort of thing so we young-sters avoided him.

So, at eight thirty, in the darkness of the narrow lane lit only by the light from a cottage window, came the dark shape of R... himself, slow and silent as he moved past the doorway in which I stood with fast beating heart lest I be seen.

He passed me by and I mewed loudly with the cry of a cat, almost bursting into hysterical laughter as R.. suddenly paused. No doubt the sudden cry had startled him in the dark-ness but then he moved on, only paces now from the boxes and his hoped for pheasants.

As he reached up to take the topmost box there was the most awful groaning and wailing noises and all the boxes 'leapt' about and fell around Rs head, even I jumping though I was part of the plan.

With a terrific shout R.. flailed out at the boxes then turning he was running past me shouting at the top of his voice...

"You horrible boys, I'll have the lot of ee, just you see, I knows all your names!" and he was gone from sight still shout-ing and raving. Jack, Tom and I swiftly tidied up the boxes amidst much chortling and went our separate ways homeward.

For years after, whenever I saw R... again I recalled the incident with some delight. Tom and his wife are still about and I hope they read this with a smile.

On one occasion along the Yeo River we watched three men gaffing fish in the weir pool and I was told that they were brothers who often fished here and it was best to leave them be. He had once shown me men 'pranging' fish in the Taw at low tide with long poles with a rake-like set of prongs at one end. They simply jammed the pole into the riverbed as they walked and took whatever flounders or other fish they caught on spikes.

Jack said he never used prang or gaff. Looking back to those days I realise he must have absolutely enjoyed pitting his skills against the wild creatures he and his family ate.

We once met two men with guns along the Yeo river. I recall them as dark in every way, their skin and clothing. They passed us without a word or even a nod as Jack said they were 'gippos' which I later learned was another term for gipsys. He said they would shoot anything and once he saw a gippo lying on a branch out over the river with his gun held vertically just above the surface, shooting salmon.

He said they would eat hedgehogs baked in clay but he never fancied that though he had eaten badger hams and even curlews when the winter was hard. He explained that at such times the farmland was a bit quieter for hunting and he went to the river with two friends for wigeon and curlew, birds which came to North Devon in vast numbers in the autumn and winter and which were much prized by wildfowlers.

It occurred to me after I had known Jack for some time that we did not seem to catch many fish, or more to the point go fishing that often and when I asked him about it he laughed.

"Ah well, I expect I catches a lot more fish than ee sees boy, but I'm up in the mornings, up with the lark".

Seeing my puzzlement he told me that quite often he pegged out lines along the river using wooden pegs and dark coloured line which he would buy in Rowe's shop in the Barnstaple High Street. Baiting the lines with choice worms he would go back in the early hours of the next day to see what might be on the end of them.

Rowe's shop, Next to the Victoria Hotel (Victoria Chambers) in the High Street was every boys favourite shop for it had stuffed birds, animals and fish of all kinds in the window, Mr Rowe being a skilled taxidermist and an expert in the ways of all field sports. I wonder how many poachers were customers of his or indeed how many hotels and inns in the area took in trout and salmon at their back doors! And still do, for there must be a market for the poachers of today somewhere.

Long before I had really delved into the lore of birds from books Jack taught me much of their ways.

Along one waterway we branched off at a mill leat and wandered up behind the mill to the millpond. There came the metallic sound of a moorhens alarm call and a flurry of water as it took off to hide in the reeds. I have always loved the way they 'run' along the water surface with wings flapping and I asked if we could stop awhile and watch them.

Jack nodded assent and we moved along to some alder trees where we sat at a distance that would not upset the birds. Sure enough within a few minutes a moorhen emerged from the dense vegetation surrounding the pond and swam jerkily towards the bank.

"There's its nest", Jack said and I saw the large hummock of a nest close to the bank yet not visible to anyone passing at that spot.

It looked large to me and yet the bird was busily engaged pulling up more vegetation and rapidly building the nest higher and higher.

"Ah, tis gwane to rain boy as sure as we're sitting yer", Jack said, "the bird knows tis gwane to rain".

And sure enough the next day the heavens opened and it rained as if it would never rain again, for the whole day. On the following day it was sunny again and as I had no arrangement to meet up with Jack I revisited the millpond.

There sitting proudly on her nest was the moorhen, the waters of the pond lapping around her and everywhere reeds flattened by the storm. She had sensed the forthcoming rain with senses we probably have but have lost touch with and her nest was safe. I've seen it happen several times since at various lakes and ponds and mostly when skies are blue and rain seems far away.

4

About Hares & Rabbits

I did not see Jack for a few days but used to wander the usual haunts wondering where he had got to until one evening there he was along the road where we'd first met up.

He had been layering a hedge for a nearby farmer and in fact I discovered as I got to know him better that he was often called upon for various farm work of this nature when regular farmhands were busily engaged about their business and when sickness and such-like meant a farm was short-handed.

Jack had served his five or six years in the army during the war, at Salerno and had been involved in the Dunkirk rescues, and had not found regular work since coming out but over the years I knew him be became increasingly busy about a variety of short term jobs.

He showed me the layered hedge and said the job was useful in more ways than one as he had been able to learn the lay of the land better on the farm. The farmer was actually moaning about having too many rabbits about, Jack explained to me, so he was going to lower their numbers a bit.

"A nice still evening is what we need boy, dry and still for the rabbits don't like rain and bolt better so we'd better go and look around tonight I think!"

On that evening we followed the stream through the valley bottom to where there were some rather flat fields with woods along one side.

Here Jack showed me a gap in the hedge where he said a hare regularly ran through. The hare would run across the open field and leap the last six to eight feet to the hedge so as to avoid leaving a trail for predators.

"Never one for hares meat myself, dark and bloody stuff and too strong I call it", Jack said.

He went on to explain that only the rich could afford to jug or roast a hare in the proper way. Years later I learned the 'proper way' was with plenty of stock, a glass of claret, lemon juice, butter, cloves and onions, peppercorns, bay leaves, parsley, red currant jelly etc. No wonder that country folk ate rabbit and anyway, they tasted better when simply cooked as well as being far more plentiful. As for me my love of hares has lasted a lifetime.

"They say tis lucky to meet up with a hare and p'raps tis true for I've had some good days when I've seen 'em. But then, I suppose I see 'em a fair bit anyway", Jack mused.

By now a shroud of mist had risen along the hollow where the footpath ran across the fields and we moved up out of its dampness to better see the lie of the land.

"Dusk and dawn are the best times for the rabbit boy, dimpsey time and Tim'll know his job better than most I reckon".

I asked Jack if he ever used ferrets and he replied he never had as it needed two men to work ferrets properly. He said he didn't want the bother and it was better to use the purse nets and rely on your dog.

Walking the wood edge Jack told me how some poachers and huntsmen he knew of were extremely cruel to their dogs and ferrets.

"Awful people, they say some people are like animals but no animals are as cruel as people boy, you mark my words".

I learned that some ferreters, moochers he called them, stitched the lips of their ferrets together to prevent them from biting the rabbits and how others broke off their fangs. To train a dog to keep quiet some beat them unmercifully and some even cut off the ends of their tongues. I now own a dog, a 'rescue' dog treated in this way by a previous owner, that is beaten, and it takes a year or more to gain their confidence fully and to restore their dignity.

"Awful people", he muttered again and the memory of these stories often come to mind today when I see dogs which cower from their owners. All you need is a steady dog and reward it when it does as ee asks it. Must ev a good nose and be able to run off 'ome when ee tells it to just in case of trouble".

We were now in a sloping field with a spinney on one side with no hedge between clumps of bramble all about at one end. I could hear water rushing nearby and knew a weir and stream lay hidden by alder trees to our left.

"Now watch Tim", Jack said and the tough little terrier trotted across the field sniffing along the bramble clumps until he suddenly stopped, pointing with his nose into one bush his body held rigid and trembling.

Jack quietly moved to the bramble bush and draped purse nets carefully but swiftly over the likely exits. He then picked Tim up and gently dropping him into the bush shouted "go and get 'em boy!" whereupon there was a hullabaloo in the bushes as Tim began barking crazily as he dashed about.

I never saw what happened in detail, saw only Jack moving swiftly to three spots where nets jerked and bulged. By the time I crossed to where the action was Jack had three rabbits in a sack and was taking the remaining nets from the bushes. Tim leapt about excitedly, probably knowing from experience the job was done and some cooked rabbit would come his way on the morrow.

Walking homeward jack explained how snares were often set for rabbits, wire snares pegged into place and quite effective. Properly made and set rabbit snares will not catch anything larger the rabbit, dying more quickly or as quickly, as when shot.

This is not to say I condone the use of snares but merely reporting the facts as I was told them. It is poor or ignorant use of them that causes cruelty for quite often if the noose is set too large an animals body will pass through. The poor creature is caught at the flanks or by one hind leg and dies in agony.

The snares set with large nooses are usually set for foxes, and may well kill foxes, badgers, cats and dogs. These are not poacher set for they would not hold a rabbit.

The rabbit was the poachers bread and butter so to speak, pheasants and other game being more a change of diet. Jack told me of gin traps.

"Terrible things and real cruel", he would say. On a few

occasions we discovered gins laid in the hedgerows and Jack would spring them with a stick and bury them deep under tree roots. Somewhere in the countryside there are quite a number of buried gin traps that will no doubt puzzle their finders as to old trapping methods. Maybe talk of giant moles will eventually enter into country legend and folklore.

5

But on to Other Matters

Just off Westaway Hill on the A39 stands a red brick house overlooking the Bradiford Valley. In my days with poacher Jack the steep sloping fields to the stream were partly covered with orchard, scores of apple trees with many plum and mazzard trees among them.

Here in apple scrumping days I was once treed with two other boys by an alsation who came from nowhere to stand with curled lips and bared fangs for what seemed hours until its owner eventually arrived. We were duly given a thrashing with a stick as apples cascaded from our bulging shirts and I for one never scrumped apples again.

One of the boys, one of the many Normans from Pilton near Barnstaple did try again by climbing up the high stone wall surrounding an orchard only to be cut about by bottle glass embedded in the cement at the summit, an old trick which was quite common in those days. He told his parents he had fallen down steps onto a milk bottle and was bandaged about the hands for some days. He is now a policeman, in fact a retired Inspector, so lessons learned....

Jack and I visited this area at times from the waterway below the orchards. We would sit under the trees and listen to the bird song and I was soon able to fit bird with song or call in several species.

He taught me to call hawks in with piercing cries that sounded exactly like buzzard, sparrowhawk or whatever, something I still do at times for the sheer pleasure of sharing a moment with one of these beautiful birds of prey.

The skies were filled with swallows, martins and swifts then, many more than one sees today and in the dimpsey bats were everywhere common. At times pheasants, tame as chicken, would pass close by us and we would just enjoy seeing it, the bronze and scarlet colours and the nearness of a bird. If Jack had had a lean time rabbiting however, he would let a pheasant pass then as it wandered out of sight under the hedge he'd be after it. In minutes he'd be back grinning and I knew he would be back later that night to collect his prize.

Jack would hide his 'ketch' in a rabbit burrow, placed at arms length and then he would jam two sticks in crossed over fashion about a foot or so inside the entrance.

"Stops the foxes and dogs having a go at it afore I do", he would explain.

He would grin as he recalled some of the times things went wrong with his 'safe' hiding places over the years.

Two or three times he'd hidden game in a rabbit burrow as I've described and when pulled out hours later the ketches had been eaten away by stoat or weasel, or rats.

"Those darn fitchees can get in anywhere", Jack grumbled, "but you should see 'ee sort out a rat, kills 'em in no time".

One day he jumped up into an old farm cart that always stood at the side of a field by Shearford Lane and never seemed to be used. He was leaving a few rabbits there for night collection when the cart took off down the slope, crashing through brambles into the stream and tipping Jack out in a heap.

Where fairly modern housing now stands along Higher Raleigh Road at Barnstaple there used to be farm buildings with a very large nursery garden filled with fruit and vegetables.

The elderly owner also kept cows and I often took them from the barns or shippons, along the road to fields across the 'New Road' as locals called the North Road out of town. Such was the lack of traffic in those days that even a young lad crossing with a herd of cattle had no need to fear accidents whereas I would not attempt it today as an adult.

Lying in the gateway to the farm were always three large wooden beer barrels and Jack told me that one morning he was walking along Raleigh (always correctly pronounced raw-lee) when he saw PC Brownscombe in the distance.

Quickly Jack deposited a number of trout he'd just caught into one of the barrels and made his way homeward, stopping to chat to the policeman on the way.

"They was for me dinner too", Jack said as he recounted the story, "so I thought they'd do for me supper instead".

He told me how he went back 'after tea' to fetch the trout and lo and behold the barrels were gone. He said he searched along the field edge inside the gate and then back along the road where a high stone wall with a huge wooden door portioned the farm area from the roadway.

There stood the landowner, the elderly farmer who I remember as always wearing tweeds, shiny riding boots and a bowler hat, a lovely old man, the Mr May who I was later to 'work' for as I explained earlier.

He said, "Evening Jack, grinned at me", said my poacher friend, "been prettying the place up a bit Jack", and the old man pointed to six huge pots of freshly planted flowers, the 'pots' made from half barrels newly sawn!

"Bin gwane to do that for years Jack and never got round to it, oh! And me and the missus had a fine tea today Jack!"

"Ee never said no more", Jack told me "and I knew what a fine tea ee'd ad alright".

For this same farmer I would sometimes spend hours filling jam jars with hundreds of cabbage white caterpillars from the leaves of his rows of cabbages and he would repay me with a bag of tomatoes from his large greenhouse.

I would be allowed to go into the sweet smelling glasshouse and pick them to take home, the small ones tasting sweeter than ever they do today. We also had the occasional perk of a dish of fresh cream which I suppose was rarity enough in the forties as so many things were.

I do recall though that my mother would put milk in a jug into a large saucepan of water on the kitchen range and keep it there boiling slowly so as to produce cream at the top. In those very early school days milk was not delivered in bottles but we would go out to the milk cart with jugs and the farmer, he delivered his own milk back then, would dip a metal container into the milk churn and fill ones jug. Bottles of milk came soon though and one of the 'honours', at school was to be appointed to milk duty which meant two of us carrying heavy crates across the playground to the various classrooms in sun, wind and rain. I remember getting into deep trouble for tripping over the top step into the school with one of these crates and hurtling thirty bottles of milk all over the corridor outside the headmaster's room. Not the sort of thing Prefects were expected to do and I think our head thought that the word Prefects was meant as a working anagram of perfect!

Another memory is of receiving my first ever banana at the age of eight just after the war. Told it was a fruit like apples and pears I promptly bit into it skin and all before being informed it should first be peeled!

Back to days with Jack.....

6

Of Rats

Rats, the brown rats, were very common in those days, especially in barns where any kind of grain crops were stored. Jack warned me many a time about them.

"Never get one in a corner or they'll leap and go for your throat", he would always say.

I remember once seeing two barn owls and a fox all taking rats which the fox had put out from an old shippon, a strange sight, the three predators hunting together in the twilight.

Many is the time I've climbed trees to look into a buzzard's nest and found a dead rat, or half a rat on the nest ready for the bird to return and resume its meal.

The hawks and owls still do a wonderful job of keeping down the rat population, Jack always maintained that rats were clean animals really and only became dangerous from a disease point of view when living near man and his sewage.

One afternoon he asked if I wanted to see a strange sight at Major Ts, a landowner residing near Westaway.

"You'll have to stand where I say and keep ever so still", Jack said, "and the Major'll show ee some rats".

Jack had obviously arranged all this in advance as when we arrived at the Majors he was waiting and took us down to a barn close to one of the old mills in the valley. I was told to stand on an old armchair placed beneath the one window of the building and to look inside. Jack stood beside me as the Major went inside and closed the door. He sat on straw piled in one corner and putting his hand to his mouth made strange squeaking sounds by sucking on the outer part of his hand between thumb and finger.

Suddenly I saw a rat move across the barn floor and I remember well trying to get off the chair to put distance between me and the barn. Jack whispered to stay where I was, keep still and just watch. I did, spellbound, as more movement showed three rats on the floor of the barn, one already at Major Ts feet and another crawling along his leg.

The Major continued making the noises. Within minutes he had six or eight of the animals moving over him and eventually there must have been a dozen or more. Some actually sat on his shoulders nuzzling his neck just as a kitten will do.

As long as I live the memory of this strange sight will remain vivid. How the Major ever learned the knack I'll never know. I never knew Jack to try it and as for me the barn was one I did not visit again ever even though I've been into score of others since and suppose they all have similar inhabitants. The fear of the unknown is often less strong than the fear of the known.

Much of what I learned with Jack was not so much of his doing but more his explanations of the things we saw on our travels.

Quite early one morning when the fields were wet with dew we were walking along a woodland path just inside the wood edge which overlooked steep meadows filled with buttercups, I remember it well as I wore my first ever rubber boots or Wellingtons, gained after much pestering of my parents who must, by then have been fed up with a lad who kept coming home with wet shoes, when my 'townie' brothers remained immaculate.

We had been watching a family of Jays raucously calling as they moved through the trees before us telling all of our presence. Movement on the hillside caught our attention and we saw the farmer, a tall very pleasant man we knew quite well by sight walking along the meadow with a cat under one arm and a gun under the other.

"He's never going to shoot the cat is he?" I remember asking Jack but he just shook his head and motioned me to be quiet. At the end of the meadow was a stand of trees, some twenty or more in a circular group, a place we often sat up in to watch the valley. The farmer made for that and we watched as he stopped to rest the cat down and then tie it to the hole of a thin sapling at the edge of the trees. He then went into cover and was lost to our view. Jack tapped my shoulder and pointed at the ground without a word and we sat close to the bushes to watch. We had become used to each others signals by now and few words were needed between us, for instance I knew to stop walking when he did or to crouch or move into cover as soon as he did so, a bit like a shadow in a way I suppose.

We could see the cat clearly from where we sat. It looked about and then sat licking one forepaw as if this was the usual morning routine.

A few minutes must have passed in this way and then I heard crows calling as several came over the trees to wheel and craw loudly over the cat who promptly flattened to the grass as they swooped over.

Suddenly there were two shots from the trees and crows dropped into the field close to the feline as the others made off rapidly over the trees.

"There, now you've seen a bit of crow baiting you wont see very often boy. Ee knows 'is business does that chap. Gets the crows when they're nesting, I spect ee knows they've got eggs so what with the crows being shot some of the eggs'll addle and ee'll gain both ways".

It was an interesting lesson of country ways and though we had witnessed rook shoots where guns fired up into the rookeries from below this was the first time I had seen a decoy cat being used. In fact when the farmer freed the cat it pranced about his heels as he wended his way back to the farm just like a kitten and obviously none the worse for the noise of close-to shooting.

On another day in that area when we were close to the farm outbuildings Jack pointed out a row of crows and other creatures hanging on the wall of the barn as if in warning that this was no place for 'pests' to be.

It was in this same valley, not far from Pudnor Woods, that we used to walk a long, winding lane which gave excellent views over the surrounding countryside.

Here Corncrakes would call in those days and we found their summer nests by searching the area where the male bird called. Now the Corncrake is a very rare nester indeed but then, when they were more common the nest was not that difficult to find in the meadows for they were usually in the smallish nettlebeds along the field edge, often with the same sort of canopy of living stems that the partridge has over its nest.

Usually the bird would scream when we were 'getting warm' and that would give the game away. Not that we threatened the nest or eggs in any way, Jack would just show me the situation and the eggs and then we would leave.

What I would give nowadays to find them so commonly. Back then I guess none of us dreamed how rare so many species of wild creatures were about to be and once gone there is little one can do about it except protect habitat and hope.

While collecting rabbits from a number of snares set along the field edge of this lane one morning we saw a fox, or the rear end of a fox at one of the spots Jack usually pegged a snare. My first thought was that the fox had been caught but then I remembered how Jack always set them too small for foxes, just right for rabbits as he would say.

Of course, as the reader may have guessed, this particular fox was making a meal of the rabbit and from what was left after it ran off it had enjoyed its breakfast.

Jack explained that probably the rabbit was fairly freshly caught and its calling could have attracted the fox for they will usually investigate such sounds. In fact I've seen a fox taking a rabbit from a weasel immediately after the little predator had caught it screaming with terror. On that occasion the fox made off across the field dragging both rabbit and weasel until the weasel was forced to release its hold.

Over the weeks of that beautiful summer there were a number of occasions when rabbits had been eaten but Jack would only grin at the competition and said very little against any wild creature.

At times Jack would take two from any clutch of moorhens eggs we found and they were very common birds along the waterways. When I queried why only two out of what was usually a clutch of six eggs he explained that you must look to the future and this years brood may be next years egg providers.

Moorhens eggs were a delicacy in many a country house in those days and one lady in the big house in a village near Barnstaple would actually ask Jack to collect them for her once or twice a year when she had friends staying.

Back then I thought little of this but I recall it with some amusement now and doubt very much if she told anyone that the source of supply was the local poacher.

There must be a joke about poached eggs....

Jack and I went on numerous mushroom gathering trips, often very early in the morning just after dawn. My parents were fond of fried mushrooms and no objections were raised at my early risings and disappearances especially when results were fruitful, or fungiful rather.

It was some time before I realised that mushrooming jaunts gave Jack an excellent idea of what else was going on in area. He would stand at field gate or gap in hedge carefully view the surrounding countryside, knowing the meaning of every track and sign and, too, how some might benefit his poaching.

I learned to walk where the cover was best and always to close gates as only rarely did we return via the same routes and Jack never visited a site on two consecutive days. There were of course many times when we were caught out in the rain which Jack did not like one bit; not that I was particularly fond of it.

In one woodland he'd made a rough shelter within a huge holly bush even to the extent of having two sheets of galvanised iron as a roof. Many a time we'd sit there and talk about the woods and woodland life, usually animals and birds for Jack seemed to know less of the wildflowers other than the commoner ones and certain herbs he would pick for culinary uses.

Often I'd come here on my own for the shelter was an excellent hide for watching wildlife from. Jack had gone to the trouble of slatting branches to make walls at the sides and all in all it was surprisingly snug inside even when pouring with rain. The woodland was situated in such as way that on the windiest of days the wind whistled through the higher canopy of the trees yet rarely affected the 'lower third' as it were.

One Easter holiday after a break of one or two weeks of bad weather I discovered a wrens nest within the shelter containing eggs. Eventually the young fledged successfully, remaining dry throughout all weathers. No fools these little birds!

Other shelters we regularly used included a linhay at the edge of a wood; the loft in a barn which we shared with barn owls, a traditional site used by the species to this day; and a small cave like hole cut into the bank of a disused quarry.

A fox once took the latter over for a while and we often found remains of prey scattered about the entrance though only occasional glimpses of the fox itself as it was usually well aware of our approach.

From the linhay shelter one winter's day we were about to move off after a shower of rain had ceased when we heard screeching noises close at hand. Suddenly, right in front of us there was commotion of sight and sound as a barn owl brought a snipe to the ground only yards from where we stood. Whether it had had come close upon the bird by surprise or chased it I do not know, or maybe the snipe had been weak from hunger for it had been a cold time but at the time Jack seemed very surprised by the incident, snipe being very swift of flight and adept at dodging about in the air.

Moments after it had killed its prey the barn owl was off, lifting the snipe into the air with ease as it winged low across the meadow like some ghost of a bird rather than flesh and blood.

Owls will have a go at almost anything when hungry or feeding their young ones. I have seen them flying by with a hedgehog on more than one occasion and once a barn owl with a stoat hanging still kicking, from its merciless talons.

A farmer who often contacts me re odd sightings in the countryside told me of finding a dead barn owl with a dead buzzard lying locked together in the middle of a field, again in winter. These birds must have fought to the death either over some prey they both wanted or perhaps one found the other weak but not yet dead in the field and attacked it too early.

I've only had one owl have a go at me and that was a barn owl. I'd reached up to grasp the floor of a barn loft to lift myself up. As my head appeared over the rim so I saw the owl launch itself toward me from where it had three young ones. I immediately let go my grasp but not before I felt the talons draw across the knuckles of one hand and I left that barn a little quicker than usual. Entirely my own fault of course and a lesson well learned is the lesson from experience rather than just being told.

Jack told me he'd had his hat knocked off a few times in his life but only when the owls had young. Otherwise they would fly out of the nearest window or other opening at ones approach and I've always found this to be true over the years. Rarely does one even see them leave a building. When checking sites in more recent years I've found it wise to have someone stand at some distance outside so that when I walk in. the other observer sees the owl leave.

To give the reader some idea of the grip of an owls talons I had a tawny owl brought to me covered in oil a couple of years ago. The bird had fallen into a large drum of oil at an industrial site and the very concerned workmen had rushed it to me hoping to save it. The owl was a sorry sight and appeared very ill so I quickly began cleaning it, finding that the particular type of oil came off very quickly with warm water and Fairy Liquid. Luckily the bird had no oil around the face area so its eyes and bill were clear of the stuff.

Suddenly as I transferred it from a lying to an upright position to clean its back the bird opened its eyes and looking at me gripped the inside of my palm with its talons, reminding me that in my haste to help it I had not put on my gauntlets!

The pain was excruciating. I found that no way could I prise its talons open with my other hand and I saw little spots of blood appear around its claws. What the heck are you doing I thought, here I am trying to help and this is what I get! I realised it was no use fighting it and went and sat down in the garden with my captor. I just sat there, very still, in agony and waited. It was twenty minutes and more before I felt the bird releasing its grip and longer before I dared risk pulling my hand away. In the end I was free and setting the owl down I dashed to the first aid kit. On my return, with a very   swollen hand, I found the bird had flown off, the cleaning job obviously enough to allow it to fly again. But be warned....

Jack was always ready to defend the predators of the wild and why not, most of them do a darned good job in keeping down creatures we consider pests and vermin.

"Foxes with cubs will bring in six or seven rats a day", he told me, "Watched 'em many a time boy, and they'll eat the lot 'cept the tails. I've gone to the earths and counted the tails mesel, so I knows tis right".

"Weasels is the boys for rats", he once told me, "They'll run into a barn swarming with the varmints and take a rat weighing more'n a pound an' and quarter with no trouble".

With weasels weighing around four ounces and rats being pretty tough beasts themselves it just shows what a fierce character the weasel really is, and of course they take a full grown rabbit with ease.

"I've seen an otter take rats up by Derby Mill, (Roth's Mill), always pigs kept up there and the rats love the place though tis a perilous place to live for a rat with foxes and owls about boy".

"I've seen a badger in the yard there eating the food out of the pig trough when the weather's hard of an evening, and if an old sow catches sight of 'em there's hell to pay... the pig'll go mad".

He went on to tell me how he himself had been attacked by pigs in his time and how touchy they can get.

"They'll shove their nose under a fence and lift it out of the ground, posts and all if they'm mad enough. Never hang about when one of them pigs is upset boy, worse than a bull."

"Me own fault I spose" he'd say with a wry grin, "should always sort out the lay of the land afore you walks on it".

He laughed at some suddenly remembered incident and told me how he was once coming into a farmyard area where pigs were often loose and 'a bit touchy' when a tramp who often wandered this area also came into view.

"There's the man to test the ground for me I thought to meself", Jack said, "so I crouched down to tie up a bootlace so's ee could pass in front and get to the farmyard first".

"Blow me if ee didn' stop just behind me so I turned to see what was up. The old devil looked at me and said ee'd let me go in first as the pigs in there could get a bit nasty sometimes".

As for bulls in fields they seem about as rare as the corncrake these days but they were common enough when I was a boy. I have actually been chased and hit by a bull and it is a most frightening experience. I was not touched by its horns at all but must have been lifted by its nose for I remember running away, the thunder of hooves and the snorting and then the blow, which did not hurt, and the landing over the hedge amongst the thorns and nettles, which did.

Bulls are funny devils, like some dogs they'll let you get well across a field beyond the point of no return and when you're full of confidence that all is well they'll be after you. And yet I've crossed fields with bulls scores of times when the most they have done is lift their heads to stare. Maybe it is the way one moves which aggravates them at times, or if they haven't had a girlfriend for a while... All I can say is only twice have I been chased and the second time I swerved away to one side to leave the animal charging down a slope and me haring over a gate.

But as I've said, some dogs are like that. I once went up to a farm door to knock and ask for a drink of water, a ploy of Jack's to see who was about.

A small terrier lay in the yard nearby, rumbling in its throat as I passed gingerly by it. It let me be however and lay there as I stood under the porch and knocked. There being no answer I walked away, passing the dog which did not even raise its head but some two paces later I felt a sharp nip in the leg and the little blighter had drawn blood and chased me the rest of the way off the premises. Geese too, are some of the best watchdogs on a farm and Jack told me how several times he'd been put to flight " by the fuss and nipping of the beasts".

I remember on one farm at harvesting time we were passing a gateway when the farmer shouted "What be ee about then?" and when Jack shouted back "nothing much" the farmer said "Well come in and give us a hand with the haymaking then".

We spent all that afternoon and well into the evening

making hay, a thoroughly enjoyable experience repeated for several years after. Rabbits would run every which way and during a break we all sat sipping cider from stone jars or pitchers, something one rarely if ever sees today.

Treasured memories are those, and too the sight of a buzzard hawk swooping down onto a small rabbit to carry it off from the hayfield, to any schoolboy like some great eagle and indeed it is a magnificent bird.

As well as rabbits there were the scores of mice and voles running about the field, harvest time being one of the best times to see small mammals in the wild.

It was all a matter of learning. A few days later Jack took me back to where the field was row upon row of stooks, the subject of many a countryside artist, and gently lifting them caused many mice to run from these their favoured hiding places during the day. And so every day that passed by I was learning a little more about the countryside and its wildlife, not realising it perhaps but storing the experiences for always, and knowing how to relive them again and again by such experience.

7

More About Eggs

As readers will recall my first ever meeting with Jack
concerned eggs. Since then he had shown me many
nests and eggs of wild birds teaching me of their ways
and where and when to find them. Along the roadsides the
hedgerows were full of nests in those days, a nest every thirty
or so paces it seemed.

Today this is not the case, due largely I think to the huge
increase in traffic, people pressure and pollution. Birds and
other creatures have moved deeper into the countryside to
nest and who can fault them. But as for Jack the only eggs I
ever saw him with were for eating though he told me he still
had an egg collection from his boyhood days.

In one valley where we spent much time the hedges were
thick and growing from hedgebanks, the typical Devon hedge
as it is now called. Here one Sunday morning..... I remember
it was a Sunday for we later sat and listened to Pilton Church
bells pealing away, the sound carried on the wind across many
a valley as it still does.....I learned more about the patience of
the man and the whiles of his kind. We were at a farm gateway
close to a weir, a lovely 'corner' where four hedges met under
elm trees and cattle always stood in the shallows and shade.

"In yer boy" Jack said and literally stepped up into the
hedge to disappear from view. I followed him into the gap Jack
had made by pulling aside some vegetation and found myself
in a world I later came to spend scores, nay hundreds of hours
in when on my own.

The hedgerow stretching before me was a corridor of green,
such a delight as any schoolboy or girl could ever wish to see...
Along the covered pathway of greenery were patches of
brighter colour where the sun shone through less dense areas

of hedge. Here and there along the route saplings and the roots and boles of larger trees showed as pillars along the way and with the 'ceiling' of dense hawthorn, hazel and other shrubs all in leaf it was a magic place to me.

We sat for a while just looking about as Jack explained he hid here many times 'when the wrong folks were about' and had suddenly hit on the idea of gradually using the hedge interior.

For weeks he had secretly cut his way along the hedgerow removing obstacles as he went, then along the next hedge and so on. That day I was amazed to find we crawled around several fields and by crossing a leat, entered another hedge to arrived in the valley woods, and all invisibly other than to the wildlife.

As we moved along this fascinating new world Jack would point out nests of Blackbird, robin, thrush, and wren. We even looked in upon a sitting hen pheasant who turned her head on one side to gaze up with one eye at the intruders in her domain. She remained on her eggs and we moved quickly on rather than disturb her. Nearer the farm the free ranging hens would often lay in or below the hedges and I discovered this was where Jack often came for eggs, and no doubt for Christmas poultry.

On one May mid-afternoon we watched a large bird alight on a small nest, remaining only so briefly that it was pure luck we saw it. Jack explained the bird was a hen cuckoo and it would have laid an egg in the hedge sparrows nests. Sure enough there in the nest of clear blue eggs was a larger egg of lesser blue. To my dismay Jack tossed it out but he then explained the ways of the cuckoo., justifying his actions by saying 'the hedge sparrows' got enough to do raising her own young without the great lout of a cuckoo to feed'.

Today my own opinion is that the cuckoo is a part of nature just as was the poacher. The cuckoo has not changed its way of life and probably has a part in nature to play that we little understand. As for the poacher in this day and age he, or more accurately, they, exploit all in their way for personal gain, but more about that later.

It was some while before I learned that cuckoos have specific hosts for the raising of their young and that there are meadow pipit cuckoos and willow warbler cuckoos and so on, the cuckoos laying eggs which closely match the colours of the host species. The hedge sparrow is of course the Dunnock or Accentor, the hedge sparrow name sticking from many years ago though the bird is not a sparrow at all.

And so in this valley Jack could move unseen, visiting field corners and the woods without putting a foot into the fields if needs be. Many a time we'd sit and just gaze out across the valley to the stream and woods and often I would delight in the fun of having people chatting away beside me yet not knowing I was there.

Once I remember laughing as a woman caught herself on brambles right in front of me whilst she was picking blackberries with two children. She turned sharply on her two youngsters and scolded them for laughing at the incident. This of course each hotly denied and I had to fight against laughing again and being seen. But back to eggs.....

Jack had a sense of humour that was more that of a practical joker at times even though the result was often unknown to us. He went into a hen house in a farmyard on one occasion and swopped four hens eggs for four crows taken from a nearby nest where the farmer had shot the crows, an incident which Jack had witnessed. As to the results we never knew but we did wait up in the hedge for the farmers wife to do the rounds. She came scurrying out of the hen house with her basket and ran into the farmhouse calling her husbands name. We promptly left.

Come to think of it I wonder who got the blame. In a similar situation near a place called Plaistow a cottager with a beautifully kept vegetable and fruit garden with a huge wooden hen house at one end shouted at us to "clear off!" as we walked along the lane. Jack immediately stopped.

"What's up maister?" he grinned.

"I know you Jack S... you needn't think you are getting' near my eggs you beggar" the man said.

"Ow do ee know I ev'n ad em already?" Jack enquired quietly.

The man dropped his spade and walked quickly towards us for the hen house was close to the hedge where we stood.

"You ad'nt better ave" the man called out and vanished inside the strongly made building.

Like a flash Jack was inside the gate and back out again having fastened the bolt below the latch as the door swung closed. We moved swiftly away. Jack laughing. It was a minute or so later that we heard the heavy thumping of fists upon the door as the angry gentleman discovered his somewhat awkward position.

"I spect his missus is 'ome boy, or soon will be any road", Jack said and that was the end of it.

As I've said before he had his ways of working things out, the fox-like cunning of the survivor, leaving gates unlatched or untied on our way to a particular place only if we were coming back that way. This meant speedier movement across country with ones spoils if speed was the order of the day. On the way back through he'd latch all gates and always tied those held with cord very securely.

"Every gate between us and them may come in handy" was his motto "but they've got to be handiest to us boy".

The collecting of wild birds eggs is illegal nowadays, indeed one requires a licence to even keep an old collection under the recent laws and a good thing too.

I did meet one elderly gentleman in my wanderings who had a huge collection which included choughs eggs taken in Devon. He was showing me a swan's egg with one small hole at one end. Usually eggs are 'blown' and thus have two holes, one at each end. It transpired that he used to make one hole then place the eggs on an ant hill.

"The ants clean them out in no time" he reckoned.

I think one of the oddest things I've ever seen regarding eggs was of a finding a curlew 'sitting' at the corner of a field on high ground near Bittadon.

We had observed the birds head and extraordinary bill of some five or six inches in length moving like some waving down-curved twig as we approached it. It was one of those very still days when every slightest movement attracts the eye and it was thus the beautiful wader drew our attention to its presence.

"A curlew boy and looks like she's nesting".

As we closed in on it, it rose and running a few feet took wing with shrill cries and flew down over the field. The nest we found had eleven eggs in it, all pheasants!

We stared and looked about but there was no sign of other eggs. Jack felt the pheasants eggs and declared them warm.

"There's a rum do, er definitely flew off yer boy dindn' er?" he said.

I agreed and we moved away to a stand of trees on a rise of ground some little way away.

Shortly after we did so the curlew returned, swinging in in a wide arc to alight and move onto the eggs of the pheasant. Jack said the pheasant may have been moved off by the curlew which must have been robbed of its own eggs but it is a puzzle to this day and I have never seen it since.

That pheasants and partridges sometimes laid in the same nests we knew from experience with usually the pheasant being the second comer but this was something quite new.

8

Following the Guns

On some of our jaunts Jack carried a heavy blackthorn stick with a knob atop and which he could use to good effect. When shoots were on at Heanton we occasionally visited Poleshill Lane and the 'Triumphant Arch' area overlooking the Taw estuary, the arch being an old stone folly covered in ivy.

On these days he'd have me hide up a tree whilst he crouched in the lane, my job being to signal to him when pheasants approached from the guns. The birds had a way of zooming up over the slope from the road area and either landing in the lane or at its edge to run to cover. Jack would use his stick to have a couple of these and then we'd be away unnoticed, secreting the birds in a small quarry at the lane to be collected later.

This 'way' of the birds did not escape the notice of the shootists for long however and on our return there for another shoot four men were getting into position as we arrived. Jack told me to go back to the quarry for safety sake and to wait there for him. He disappeared into the trees as I went back as bidden, hearing shots from afar off as occasional bursts were fired. After a while there were shoots from closer to hand and soon after Jack appeared with a brace of pheasants which he hid in a hollow tree near the road.

We left Poleshill, travelling homeward via Halls Mill Lane to Pilton, Jack telling me of waiting in the trees until shot birds dropped into the area whereupon he collected them "to save the shooters avin to look for em…"

He never took Tim on these jaunts involving shooting of any kind nor when we wandered further afield than usual via a main road, in fact often when we were in a hurry he would scoop the little dog up and carry him for long distances.

One of the beaters who went on regular shoots in the area, a man called Lakeman, had a friend with a black Labrador who would be told when and where to be waiting. He would shoot a bird or two when he could do so without being seen or otherwise send his dog to pick up kills that had dropped close.

I knew of a fox which also learned this 'trick', but in more recent years in the Braunton marsh area where there is some winter wildfowling done. The fox suddenly appeared out of the reeds one Saturday morning immediately after shots had been fired and at first I thought it had been put out by the noise and disturbance. It ran to an object lying on the ground near the reed fringe and I saw it was a mallard duck as the fox ran off with it in its jaws. I watched it cross the fields and with my binocular saw where it ran into a huge gorse clump near a hedge, its prize held proudly as it ran.

Minutes later two men came into the reeds with a spaniel searched around for a while then left shouting to nearby colleagues that they hadn't found the duck. That the fox is an opportunist everyone knows but this was really a bit of class thinking on the fox's part, man providing it with a winter larder!

Foxes usually hunt singly unless the cubs are being taught in a family party, but I've seen adult foxes in pairs especially in the mating season. One of the finer sights in nature is that of two foxes wandering the countryside on a moonlit winters night with frost painting the land silver.

Once near Muddiford Jack and I came upon four foxes feeding together off a stag carcase. This may have been a family party, I cannot recall the month of the year anyway but it is a fact that foxes from a wide area may be drawn by a large kill, not of their own making of course for a fox would not tackle a full grown red deer. Jack once baited a fox with a kipper so that I could have a close look at the animal. We sat in the branches of a tree to watch, "out of the fox's nose" as Jack put it. The first to approach the bait was a magpie, which flew off when Jack lobbed a stick at it. A hedgehog also had a good sniff but decided it was not to its taste and moved on.

Eventually a fox did arrive. The strange thing to me was that I did not see its coming, it was just there, staring around and down at the bait while we watched from just yards away. It was beautiful, looking very red in the evening to a young school-boy. It bit a portion from the kipper and ate it then picking up the remainder it trotted off into the trees. I asked Jack to do the same again one night but he said he'd rather eat the kippers himself.

Talking of kippers reminds me that one morning when two or three of us boys were off to school a man appeared with a cart, shouting "Clovelly errins!" at the top of his voice. Clovelly Herrings were choice local fish and always sold as such. On this particular day, our houses being built along The Rock at Pilton and reached by steps the travelling fishmonger took a basket from door to door.

One of us three boys promptly picked up the tabby cat, which always perched in the sun at the top of one of these flights of steps and dropped it onto the cartload of fish. The cat stood there for a moment with arched back then realising its luck grabbed a bright silvery breakfast and bolted, scattering fish onto the road. We were soon in school telling of our 'adventure' to our classmates. What we did not expect was that no one had seen the cat scatter the fish onto the road so all three of us got punished for it on arrival home at lunch time, or dinner as it always was to us. It appeared that the fishmonger had complained bitterly on finding the fish in the road and we three were the only ones about at the time. A fitting sort of justice I suppose. But back to foxes and to people associated with them in one way or another....

Near one small village on the outskirts of Barnstaple lived a couple whose home was flanked by stone walls of good height. Much of the land inside these walls was tilled with vegetables and there was also a large stone building with wooden racks lining one wall, for storing apples Jack reckoned. An old green lane ran along one side of the house and it was possible to look over the wall by standing on piles of logs cut for the winter fires. Jack knew the people well and if they appeared not to be at home we would check the garden by climbing the log pile.

On one such day I stared over the wall to see movement in a large cage built against the barn. The cage had a door at one end and was a wire netting affair for most of its length but with a wooden, tea-chest sized door area at the end. The whole thing ran the length of the barn wall and was probably some twenty feet long. The movement turned out to be fox cubs, four of them, se we pushed open the door into the walled garden and went to have a look. The foxes ran for cover, cramming into the boxed end of the cage with one head then another peering out. We watched them for a while then hearing a door slam and the barking of a dog we went in search of the owner.

"Didn't think I'd see ee with foxes about the place Jimmy", Jack said to the older man who had appeared with his lurcher dog around the side of the house.

"No, don't spose you did Jack but I can get a few quid for em in the right places as I spect ee knows".

"Aye, I didn't think ee was raisin em to ev your bantams Jimmy" Jack laughed as he pointed at the little brown chicken-like fowl running about the yard.

Over a cup of tea and bread and jam sandwiches I heard the two talking of fox hunting. It turned out that Jimmy had dug out the fox cubs early in May and would release them for the hunt somewhere further afield. Jimmy caught me staring at the head of a stag on his wall, an animal with a superb set of antlers.

"Ow d'ee think I caught that'n youngster?" he enquired of me.

I shook my head as I knew little about deer hunting.

"Got'n in a snare just like your friend Jack yer gets his rabbits" and he laughed at my obvious show of disbelief until Jack verified that this was indeed the way the stag was caught and then shot in the snare.

There were badger and otter heads on the walls also and even at that early age, I was still at junior school, I decided I did not like the man and never went there again.

On the way home from Jimmy's place however, Jack told me more about the old man and his way of life and how he had been shown much of the country lore I was now learning from him in return. It transpired that Jack had been brought up into a country way of life that involved almost every aspect of hunting, shooting and fishing one could imagine and had been badger baiting and the lot.

"Not for me that sort of thing boy, but the old codger taught me a lot, owever rough ee is ee'll give ee' is last".

He told me how Jimmy used to snare pheasants at their night roosts in trees by using a wooden pole with a snare at one end which he'd reach up and drop over the pheasants neck.

He said that one night Jimmy and one of his brothers knew a farmhand had been told to sit up and catch them poaching. They had been told about this by the local pub landlord who heard about most things and was not averse to a trout or pheasant now and then. He had got the farmhand talking after a couple of ales and was able to tell Jimmy where he was going to sit up that night.

Jimmy had gone to the spot along with his snare pole and finding the man sitting in the trees with his back to the track Jimmy was on he dropped the snare over the farmhands head, "pulling it just tight enough to frighten'n a bit..." leaving the snare pole where it was.

" I bet the chap didn' go down that lane in the dark again for a while", Jack said.

Jack also told me how Jimmy's dog, the lurcher, could be let out at night on its own and could be guaranteed to come back with a rabbit for the pot.

"Nort you can do 'gainst a dog like that at night boy. Black's the ace of spades and like lightning when ee moves, nuff to give ee a turn if ee met'n in the dark that one is".

Jimmy, he said, had been caught two or three times and fined for poaching or possessing game he had no right to. This of course made him all the more cunning and he soon recouped his fines with a salmon or two.

"Ee always got money in 'is pocket, specially when the Fair comes to town, Whitelegs and Anderton & Rowlands does well out of his family", laughed Jack "and it always coincides with pheasants or salmon in the butchers shops down town, or on the board in a hotel".

The 'board' was Jacks reference to the menu and even today some are richer for fare caught in the wild by poachers. Catching the supply is only worthwhile when there is a demand.

The one and only time Jack and I saw rutting red deer in our days together was near a secluded farm surrounded by woodlands and called Slowley Barton. A farmhand had informed Jack that there were several pheasants to be had in that area, easy pickings he'd said, for the cocks were drumming just as they do in spring. Pheasants often do this, a sort of Indian summer mating with full display, the crowing and rapid wing beating of the cocks attracting hens being noticeable from a long distance.

We had entered the area via woods, seeing buzzards and sparrowhawks hunting the valley as we passed along it, walking just inside the wood edge, unseen but seeing all about us. It was a beautiful day and one in which Jack pointed out the masses of berries, "fruit for all" as he would say, "and belonging to no man and all men...."

Rowan berries, rosehips, haws, I learned them all and Jack said his wife had picked 'loads' of rosehips during the war years and that someone used to collect them for the making of rosehip syrup for children, something which my mother also did on a regular basis.

"Yer's parson in the pulpit boy, see these stalks of bright red berries all along the hedge". Red was always pronounced 'rade' and it took me a while to realise that 'yaller' was yellow. It will be a sad day when we lose the dialect words and sounds and their richness, let's hope we never do.

He explained that these were the berries of the lovely sheath-like plant of spring that carries its purplish 'club' inside it. I knew it as Lords and Ladies and was told that snakes ate the berries to obtain the poison for their fangs. Not true of course but a useful reminder that the berries are poisonous to humans. The plant is called snake-food by some country folk to this day and is the Wild Arum or Cuckoo Pint.

We proceeded along the hedgerow on the side 'away from' the nearby farm when suddenly I heard a strange roaring, all the world like lion or bear to a youngster hearing it for the first time other than in films. Jack ducked down in front of me and I really thought some wild beast from a jungle film was loose upon us and promptly did the same.

Crouching close to the hedge I moved nervously forward at Jack's beckoning and peered through a gap in the hawthorn trees: There on the hillside which sloped steeply down to the Pudnor Woods were two red deer stags and even as we watched they lowered their heads and clashed their antlers.

We could clearly hear the 'clack-clack' of thrusting antlers. I could hardly believe we were actually watching these two magnificent animals in combat, one of the most exciting but awesome sights in Nature. We must have arrived well into the dispute for the battle was short-lived, one stag turning away suddenly to canter along the hillside below us. The victor tossed his mighty head and turned away to where I realised more deer stood silently on the hillside at some distance, colours merging with hedgerow and rust coloured bracken.

All too soon they were gone, Jack explaining the reason for the 'fight' and that this was the time of the rut for these animals.

"Lots of 'em up on the moors boy", he told me "They'm fine beasts but bigger'n the likes of us wants to carry 'ome".

We watched the deer roam away over the hillside and then stood in a gateway searching the valley for pheasants as Jack chatted about deer, venison and the people who hunted them. Frankie L., was an expert with the crossbow. He lived at Derby in Barnstaple and was a crackshot Jack said. One winters Saturday night he was walking along Derby Road with a friend when they saw a holly wreath hanging on a pub door for it was close to Christmas.

"Frankie's friend bet him a pint he couldn't hit dead centre of the wreath", Jack said "so Frankie stood in the middle of the road and let fly, just as some chap opens the door to walk out. The bolt shot past the poor chaps head and vanished inside the pub. There was a terrible row after that Frankie was banned from that pub for ages. Twas a wonder the chap who opened the door did'n have a use for that wreath" Jack murmured.

"Course, he used his crossbow for deer did Frankie, not much noise you see and ee gets in another shot as easy as winkin. If you knows your deer paths you can't get'm with snares. Terrible cruel mind you but then, these chaps ain't got no feelins for what they'm after boy. There was a chap called Pinn who asked Frankie about catching deer and Frankie told'n about snares, said he could get'm by the legs or the neck if ee picked the right places. This chap Pinn tried it one night, then another and then ee got a bit impatient as ee wud'n catching nort so ee put out several wires for legs like. Next morning ee'd got a pricket in thisy so ee thought ee was a fine poacher and laid the wires out again in the same way. This is as true as I'm standing yer", said Jack, "old Pinn went away along the lane leadin to a farm when the farmer and 'is son suddenly showed up. They shouted on seeing' Pinn who panicked and turning about dashed off the way ee'd come. Blow me if ee didn't run 'is legs straight into 'is own wires and fell flat on ee's face."

"Course, ee was caught alright and ee 'ad two shiners (black eyes) and was fair cut about the face. The two farmers never reported'n to the police but those shiners didn't come from fallin down, you mark my words. Then there was Jack Westacott who met up with Pinn about a year later. Westacott was a pigeon man, raced 'em for years..... but ee never beat any", Jack roared with laughter at this joke, a favourite of his. "Well Westacott and Pinn got together in the beginning to sort out the peregrines that Jack Westacott reckoned used to get 'is pigeons. Twas true enough, you'd see the peregrines fly up over Pilton and they'd stoop on a pigeon right over 'is house while Jack shouted and swore down below. All ee'd get was a few feathers for 'is shoutin'. Anyway Pinn must'v told Westacott about catching the pricket with snares and they thought they'd ave a go together and keep a better eye out for the farmers at the same time. They went over Loxhore Cut where the deer used to come in to Collarbridge (Collard Bridge) and along the River Yeo. They set up snares along a deer path, a lane with a wood at one side and a high bank on t'other. Mark you boy this was miles from where Pinn was first caught in 'is snares and they weren't seen by a soul."

"That night there was high winds and rain and next morning early the two men went to check their snares. They got there just as twas getting light and the whole track was full of cow pats though that didn't warn them of what was to come. Suddenly they was laid into by half a dozen blokes, Westacott managing to escape with little hurt and run away but old Pinn, ee was a sorry sight again, black and blue for days, is lips so swollen ee couldn't face a pint even. D'you know" Jack said, "with the stormy weather the cows from the farm 'ad come up along the lane where they always sheltered at such times overnight, cows not being as daft as they look, and one of 'em got erself caught in a wire. Course er bellowing brought out the farmer and he was so mad ee laid the trap for the two men to teach em a lesson". Jack laughed. "When Pinn told me what 'ad happened ee said ee hoped fifty peregrines would come up over Pilton for the way old Westacott had bolted. Mark you boy I don't think ee'd ave gained a lot by staying about".

As we chatted on about these and other characters a tall sun-browned man appeared along the hedge and he too seemed to know Jack.

"Nothing much to do today then Jack?" the man enquired.

"No, why is there anything ee wants doin' maister?" Jack replied, always the soul of politeness.

"Yes, I've got a little job for you, and the boy can help too".

For the next few hours we cut and stacked logs, Jack wielding the axe powerfully as he split the logs down the middle, with me stacking neatly away against a stone wall and enjoying every minute.

A treat was in store for the lady of the house fed us well afterwards and the farmer, grinned, gave Jack a hen pheasant as his 'pay'.

"Something for the family Jack", and Jack touched his hand to his hat, well pleased with the day.

It always intrigued me as a boy, the places Jack would hide the tools of his trade. Valuable as they are to the poacher he would rarely if ever take them home. Fishing tackle he usually hid in a largish cavity beneath the arch of a bridge over his favourite fishing water. At some stage in the past stones had fallen from the archway and it was possible to reach inside where the hole was much larger than the actual entrance. Jack told me he had noticed the hole when following up salmon he was after. He now used it regularly as his 'hidey-hole'. Just a few months ago I wandered nostalgically along the same waterway to find the same hole in the old bridge, dusty and warm from July heat, but nothing more.

Snare wires were available for use at a number of sites. A milk churn with a rusted hole in its bottom rested on a stone slab in a hedge at one farm entrance and housed one set of wires. Another set hung of a nail at the corner of a Dutch barn in full view of anyone caring to look. Jack always maintained that if you 'hid' things where all could see no one ever did. A third set lay between hay bales and the wall of George Huxtable's barn where I used to help feed the pigs of an evening. This was near the top of Manning's Pit, a steep field with a wooden footbridge over the stream at the bottom where a fourth set lay in an oiled cloth laid in a hole trowel cut from the hedge. Thus Jack could move about the countryside lightly laden and free from worries, able to pick up gear almost anywhere he needed.

In a small disused quarry along a track called Smokey House Lane he kept a length of board about two and a half feet in height and some six feet in width. It was made of planks held together by stakes the points of which protruded below and could be fixed firmly into the soil.

Two 'tunnels' a foot or so in height were cut out of the bottom of the board and some distance apart. When placed across the lane at a spot "where pheasants always walk" the board made a barrier with just the two ways through. Jack would net these off and would lie up in the hedge of an evening watching for pheasants to pass. Once they did so he would hop into the lane and the pheasants would scoot off along it, find the barrier and more times than not, dive through the nearest hole whereupon they would be Jack's. Few actually took flight in this situation as Jack never raised enough noise to cause them to do so, pheasants having a way of relying on their running ability when they see no reason to do otherwise.

I think the greatest fright I ever had, far worse than being caught scrumping apples, was on a day when Jack asked me to pick up wires from a barn which stood alone in a field under oak trees. I looked carefully about me as I strolled across the field towards the old building and then became distracted by goldfinches feeding on the thistles standing tall and purple-topped about the field.

They dipped and bobbed before me in their undulating and chattering flight, perching briefly on thistle heads and twittering onwards as I closed upon them, flashes of scarlet and gold, black and white and fawn. I reached the barn which had a hole in the door which one reached to raise a metal latch on the inside in order to open it. Pushing my hand through the hole I almost passed out with shock as it was gripped by another hand! There was a roar of laughter and the door swung open to reveal the farmer with a broom in one hand.

"And what might you be about lad?" he asked grinning at what must have been one of the whitest faces he'd ever seen.

"I'm just out for a walk", I gasped knowing that Jack was two fields away waiting for me unseen.

"Well lad, you want to look where you'm gwane and go where you'm looking, you was like a lost sheep coming across the field, saw you from the window".

"Yes, sorry mister, was looking at the finches" I muttered and backed away. I looked back as I made my way out of the fields and he was still watching I went the 'wrong' way to detour back to find Jack who himself had a good laugh at my experience.

"Ee's a crafty old coot that one, we'd best leave those wires where they are for a week or two, ee's bound to wonder why you walked in there". Jack said.

"It weren't that long ago that I met up with him coming up the farm lane with two of my snares, one with a pheasant still in it that I was going to check from the night before. I always think ee saw me gwane down to set the snares the night. He stopped and said to me 'if you sees anyone who looks like they might be poaching Jack, you'll let me know won't ee'."

Remembering this incident with 'sharp' farmers brought Jack into one of his rare chat moods and he went on to tell me of how in his younger days he had learned the wisdom of never revisiting the same place on conclusive nights. There is a farm quite close to the edge of town with a good river and a weir where salmon run twice a year. Here Jack had begun 'poking about to see what there was for the catching' shortly after he had left school at the age of fourteen. Two nights following he had quietly wandered by the farm and on both occasions had a look inside an outbuilding with loads of ropes, old cartwheels, earthenware jars, bundles of wire netting and the like, "just to see what there was to see" he told me.

"On the third night I did the same, noticing the door was slightly ajar as I strolled in. There was a whoosh and the flaming great branch of a tree caught me a beauty about the shoulders and head. Fair taught me a lesson" grinned Jack ruefully.

It was the sort of 'school boy' prank type booby trap that one realises could have a devastating effect when used by an adult. Field craft is much more than merely being able to walk quietly through the countryside, it is also about interpreting the many signs one sees, indeed about SEEING.

I know many a good birdwatcher who knows his or her birds very well by sight but rarely relates what the bird is doing or why it is where it is to the bird itself. To me this is the essence of nature. Good to know a marsh tit is a marsh tit but nicer still to know what the bird is up to.

Alarm calls for example may mean that and little more to the casual observer but I like to pause awhile to observe what may be the cause of the alarm other than possibly myself. Watch a flock of sheep raise their heads to watch you as you pass by some distance away. They do not stand and stare idly, as maybe we do at times when day dreaming or just admiring the view. They watch because we might be 'trouble' or a threat of some kind.

It is the same with rabbits in a field. If they are all uneasy and keep raising themselves up to stare around it is a sure sign something is worrying them. Thus Jack taught me to observe other creatures and in a way to use their sharper senses to my advantage as well. We sat up in our hedgerow corridors one afternoon and late into the evening just watching a field of sheep. They soon 'forgot' we had moved through the hedgerow and resumed feeding as we settled back to observe.

Sure enough, after a while all heads raised and pointed to one corner of the field where a lane entered it. The sheep nearest the lane moved away and flocked closer together in the middle of the field. A man with a dog came into view, the dog on a leash, and as soon as they were some distance along the stream bank the sheep settled once more.

Heads again went upminutes later and following their gaze we saw cattle entering the next field after being released from the farm from milking. Several sheep near the stream looked to stare yet again and we watched the lovely sight of a grey heron fly low to drop onto the bank and wade into the water to fish. The sheep paid no heed once they knew what it was they had seen from the corners of their eyes and again went on feeding.

It was the heron itself which next told us of further distur-bance for with a harsh 'squark!' it launched into the air to fly upstream away from a badger that had moved out into the early evening to search for supper.

And so in these obvious yet all important ways we soon learn how better to become a part of the countryside and to wear colours which blend with ones surroundings, not to chatter away too loudly or to wave ones hands about unduly. Never smile at the birdwatcher wearing camouflaged type shirt or green and brown hat pulled down over his or her face. They are almost certainly going to see more than he or she wearing bright colours and moving about at any speed other than slow or steady. I well remember in recent years joining a field trip organised by one of the local bird groups. Some people in their twenties were nudging each other and pointing towards a middle aged gentleman wearing just such clothing and with a thumbstick, walking boots, a rucksack and his binoculars.

They were clad in bright sweatshirts and jeans with 'trainers' on their feet, shoes which I know are popular and comfortable and much used by joggers and the like. They were obviously very keen young people and carried binoculars and cameras slung about their necks, out to enjoy the day and the promise of good birding.

Two hours later from the main road, well into the wilder parts of Exmoor near the Long Stone and Pinkery Pond area they were straggling, one fellow worrying about a turned ankle and all four pairs of trainers wetly brown from trudging through the tussocky bog country and sheep tracks that is much of Exmoor. We stopped to watch ring ouzels in one of the coombes while they caught up, legs scratched by brambles which often refuse to give up their tenacious hold of other vegetation and can bring a man down with ease.

The man in camouflaged clothing eyed them quickly for a moment and then said....

"You'd get so much more pleasure out of your rambles if you wore sensible clothing... just like it suggests on your field trip programme. I was like you in my younger days but I soon learned." The young folk nodded assent quietly and looked at each other. I feel they wear sensible clothing these days.

I thought of Jack on that day. Always he wore quiet colours, he was a quiet man, and he saw more on his rambles than most; a good teacher. Of course the best way to learn is from the wild creatures themselves, from the way they go about their lives as well as from the colours they 'wear'. It is important for the predator to use stealth and cover as it is for the prey, probably moreso and even birds of prey which have very fast flight powers to catch their prey also rely on cover and other ways of approaching unseen.

Witness for example the hedgehopping hunting method of the sparrowhawk which comes upon its prey often unseen, or the peregrine falcon which will plunge 'out of the sun' to help it make its kill in mid-air. These are all skills learned from experience and though they may be said to be instinctive my feeling is that instinct itself is a learned reaction, the brain just working that bit faster than we normally employ it.

That man was a hunter in his early days cannot be denied. A hunter for meat he was, out of necessity, vegetarians would not have lived very long in our climate in those days. It is likely it is the hunting instinct remaining in us that is fostered by the various 'watch wildlife' organisations today in that given binocular or telescope we become hunters once again, if only to see or at the most shoot our quarry with cameras. Witness the ornithologist stalking wading birds or wildfowl on a lonely marsh, binocular at the ready, creeping through reeds and rushes using all available cover until at last he crouches, silently focussing snipe, wigeon or whatever...

There you see the hunter of old, and of today, but with a happier end result for the hunted. Good hunting.....

9

National Service Wildlife

M y two and a bit years in the R.A.F were spent mostly in Bomber Command, with the last few months in the Fleet Air Arm on attachment. Goodness I could tell some stories about those days but I'll hold to the nature watching aspects.

Any action I saw was mainly in NAAFI queues and the daily battle for coffee and buttered rolls, sheer bliss! It was the 1950s and the times of Suez and Aden. I was stationed at two camps in Somerset, Weston Zoyland and Merryfield, following training at Padgate and Hereford. I must admit that although I was a Westcountry fellow, when I had my posting to Weston Zoyland I thought I was off to Holland, not to the lovely land of cider apples and Somerset Levels.

We had Canberras on camp, and later some Meteors, for photographic training I believe, and then V Bombers so security was tight. I recall well chaps I served with, Alan Greer, Keith Baker, Cyril Olds and our delightful 'Squaddie' Leslie, a Scot, and his Flight Lieutenant Etheridge, the latter an England Hockey Player. I took a camera back to camp one weekend but was told I couldn't use it on or around the camp. However we finished work at 4pm which meant long summer nights on the Levels watching otters and other wildlife and back then there was a lot of it about. A woman in a cottage at the outskirts of Ilton Village showed me all the best places. She had excellent binoculars so we'd take a pair each to a delightful river and stream area with willows, lanes and wooded areas. I think I saw more wildlife during those times than anywhere.

We were one of the early camps to have long weekends, finishing Friday afternoons until Mondays. Alan and I discovered that if one volunteered for Camp Patrol on a Thursday night, we'd be given Friday off which was very useful all year round. Camp Patrol was the all night security patrol wandering around the camp perimeter which on a bomber drome with its huge runways was quite a long wander. So, we'd go to work on Thursday, have tea, then go straight on to Camp Patrol throughout the whole night. Around 2am in the morning we'd be allowed into the mess where a Duty Sergeant would give the nod and we would do a huge fry up of eggs, bacon, fried bread, tomatoes and anything that was going, along with gallons of tea or coffee. We ate well. And the night wildlife we saw was amazing, barn, tawny and little owls, fox, badger, otters, our powerful torches picking out every movement. Then off duty around 6 am, on to breakfast at 6.30 am and off home with a 72 hour pass until Monday. Or we would just stay on camp and wander the countryside.

There was a fellow called Don, a civvy on the camp who was a true countryman and Westcountryman. As soon as he heard my Devon accent we became good pals and he, too, would tell me where to find otter holts, badger setts and such around and about the camp and village. Our Squaddie, the Squadron Leader in charge of our section was a friendly Scot and as long as work was done he'd tell us to 'clear off' and away to the countryside I'd go, with Hattie sorting out some food beforehand. She was into herbs from the wild for medicinal and culinary uses so I learned a great deal from her, and she was also a great folklorist, knowing all the local haunted and fairy places around and about. Hattie was some twenty years my senior, a white witch, very popular in the area when people and livestock needed healing, so I learned much at the hands of this charming and learned woman.

Alan and Cyril went occasionally to look at the wildlife but they were more interested in two younger ladies of the area, especially Cyril who had a 'Dear John' letter at mail call one day. He went off the rails for a while but we soon straightened him out. The comradeship of the Services was quite something. I look back on it now with only memories of the happy times.

Hattie who had her own small cottage on the outskirts of the village showed me the secrets of the Somerset countryside just as Poacher Jack had done in my formative years, making my RAF days fly swiftly by. A person greatly missed is she, yet always around I feel.

Back then the Somerset Levels and countryside all around teemed with wildlife, the large camp and the tight security helping many a species I'm sure even though nature conservation back then was simply part and parcel of the good old traditional farming carried on throughout the countryside as the way of life for the rural community.

The 1950s were, though, the times of myxomatosis in rabbits, DDT and other pesticides showing up by destroying many raptors, and the spread of mink from fur farming escapes and releases, the beginnings of the declines and sad moments that have faced wildlife species ever since. The times were changing and not for the better.

As I have said, the events appertaining to nature watching in my life are not set down here in chronological order but more as a wandering through my memory, reminiscing if you like.

When the Fleet Air Arm took over our camp at Merryfield all but eight of us RAF personnel were posted away to other parts. At least I think it was eight, give or take one or two. Life changed dramatically, the food was immediately better than we had had previously. There were choices and menu boards to choose from in the Mess, urns of coffee, tea and other drinks to help ourselves to. There were blue eiderdowns with anchors stitched on each on every bed and the 'bull' was stepped up again almost to the extent of our original training camps. We few RAF chaps were virtually aliens, all the moreso because we were National Service wallahs soon to be demobbed. We weren't really integrated, more ignored but well looked after in terms of food and accommodation along with that segregated feeling.

It didn't bother me a bit, nor Alan Greer. Cyril would get disgruntled in his tough Hull manner and a chap called Bill B from South Devon somewhere, walked right into trouble from the start. Bill's parents ran a pub so he always went home at weekends, as I often did as we both lived in the Westcountry.

Ilton had a tiny railway station, built I suspect because of the

RAF camp. It was a Halt, a stopping place for trains to and from Taunton and nothing more so one would walk a mile or so down the road, get on a train, then get off at Taunton to buy tickets to wherever one was going. And so the weekend jaunt along the road in spring and summer was a lovely part of the journey we had all gotten used to, a mile long traipse, a country walk in fact.

O n our first weekend as Fleet Air Arm, Alan and I had gone off in the early morning from Camp Patrol, leaving a camp just awakening to the day. Bill's story was told to us by the grim moody Bill himself a couple of days later. He had left camp without reading the new Standing Orders, well, almost left. When a couple of hundred yards along the road he said a screech of brakes and two Military Police had swerved their vehicle in front of him. Bill was asked if he was blind to which he said no with some amazement. He had not saluted the Yard Arm was the first complaint, and had foolishly asked what a Yard Arm was. A new addition to the camp entrance near the Guard Room was pointed out to him, comprising white painted ropes, a bell, and a boom across the road. The Yard Arm was part of 'the ship' we were now on and had to be saluted on entering and exiting the camp, or 'ship'. We were of course many miles from the sea and the concept of being on board a ship was difficult for us to understand, especially as we'd been on camp much longer than the Fleet Air Arm. They had arrived with us, by the way, because the runways at Yeovilton were breaking up and extremely dangerous and would evidently take an age to repair.

Anyway Bill had ignored the Yard Arm which I must admit Alan and I had forgotten even though we had acquainted ourselves with the rules, for we had left through a hole in the fence as we often used to use as a short cut.

Bill was also asked why he had not gotten into the 'Liberty Boat' instead of trying to walk off the ship. It appears Bill then put his foot further in the mire by saying 'what bloody Liberty Boat?' It transpired that this was the coach parked by the road-side to take personnel to the train, from the ship! Bill, literally all at sea, had then groaned at the two MPs, 'blow the Liberty

Boat, I'll bloody swim ashore".

"Not his weekend you wont", he was then told and he spent two days in the Guard Room cleaning the already spic and span building.

And so our indoctrination into the Fleet Air Arm was established and Alan and I determined to begin 'clearing' in readiness for our demob. But that's another story.

Really I remain grateful to the Royal Air Force and the Fleet Air Arm for having camps in Somerset in what was the best of wildlife country and in some ways I regret not signing on for a full time tour of duty.

10

Moving On

Demobbed and now a young man in my twenties my own first binocular was a Zenith 7 X 50, a heavy Russian made instrument of considerable strength that could be banged against gates with no real risk if one was climbing over. To me they were the absolute dream glasses and I was rarely without them. The light gathering power was excellent and I'd reverse them to use them as a 'microscope' to see wild-flower close ups and such, something few binocular owners seem to be aware of. Just turn them the 'wrong' way over the subject close to, then look down into the object lens and you have an excellent magnifier for viewing close up details.

So what to do to learn more. Perhaps wander the fields, lanes and woods to see what's about then read up on it, or set myself some kind of target to be sure I got around more. I settled for the latter. As it turned out it was one of better decisions in my life. My target was to see, in a breeding situation, all the birds of North Devon, which virtually meant 'the Westcountry', as North Devon comprises such a mix of habitats and has many areas for adult birds to be nesting and feeding young, that is carrying food to them. Birds carry food about for young usually, not to eat it themselves later. Certainly this applies to those seen in the breeding season which is basically from late March to September some species raising two or three broods. This project offered me the Spring and Summer to observe and achieve my objective; about 5 months of the year roughly.

To my mind as one who had the gift for finding nesting birds, the patience taught me by Jack, along with good old fashioned field craft from my days with him it seemed a perfectly reasonable ambition. Little did I know it was to take me over four years and into beautiful countryside some of which I feel sure that the 'white man' had never trod, as they say in the old tales of exploration. Exploration it was, from the easy nest finding of blackbirds and mute swans to the sheer excitement of red backed shrike and yellow wagtails. But I did it eventually and it is a challenge for any ornithologist today, no easy matter. Try it…

Luck played its part as any nature watcher will know. Many is the time I have been hunting for one species only to find two or three others magically show themselves with food for young. I was sitting watching willow warblers in a wood one early morning when I found wood warblers building and chiff chaffs carrying food along the same pathway. That same summer whilst watching great tits taking food into a tree hole I found redstarts, nuthatches and spotted flycatchers all nesting nearby.

The tits were fairly easy and numerous, find and follow, learning their songs. That is part of the secret, bird song so often denoting territory and then it becomes a case of sitting quietly to watch and learn. I much preferred to sit by or in a tree and use the binocular. I had moved on to the Swift Classic, fine glasses of 8X40, lighter and with excellent optics. I gave my Zenith away to someone who, like me, had never owned a binocular. They are probably still around somewhere giving someone else pleasure. I hope so. Indeed, today I use Leica 10 x 42, and I've given the Swift binocular away.

My task by the way, had to be achieved in the wild with no garden nests acceptable though I could have kicked myself a few times, especially when goldcrests nested in view of my home windows and I had the Dickens of a job finding collared doves beyond garden boundaries.

My first ravens nest came to me courtesy of Henry Williamson's 'Tarka the Otter', for I went in search of his Kronk the raven site and found it. It was a misty evening, drizzle coming in off the sea and I was getting soaked. I was sure I'd heard ravens calling in the distance and was plodding along a sheep track on the edge of a cliff with the sound of my own panting and the roar of the surf in my wet ears. I decided

I would walk as far as a stone wall showing the end of this part of the cliffs for there was then a break with a the next likely spot a mile away hidden by swiftening rain.

As I came to the cliff edge I saw the sloughed skin of an adder before me and bending down to pick it up there in over the grass sward overhang, on a sandstone ledge with the waves crashing beneath it a hundred feet below was a nest with three young ravens on it. At that moment the heavens could have opened and deluged me and I would not have cared. This was a perfect moment among many I was to find on my quest and I could see also why I had thought I heard ravens. On the very edge of the next piece of cliff was a rickety fence and there upon it were the two black hunched forms of the adult ravens watching me. I was so exhilarated at my find that I waved to them in gratitude, turned and climbed the steep slope by the wall. 'Kronk-kronk', I heard and turning saw the birds below me, one dropping to the nest the other watching over the edge.

I still have the sloughed adder skin in my den in a Delft vase, a fitting place for it, part of my memories of those times, and both valuable in their own ways.

Later, when the weather improved I went back to this traditional nest site of the ravens, taking photographs for my records. Williamson's Tarka' was written in 1923. The nest site was used up until 1993 that I know of but erosion and cliff falls occurred there one winter and I have not been back recently.

And here I must digress for a moment. As well as in 'Tarka' the site was well recorded for posterity. Some years ago when I had become known for my interest in wildlife I did some location finding for the BBC Natural History Unit at Bristol who were wishing to film 'Beyond The Edge', the story of wildlife of coastal cliffs. The ravens were perfect for the film and one morning at 3am I crept in darkness along the cliff edge with my Jamie Woods portable hide and erected it whilst the birds were asleep. At 5am Andrew Anderson arrived on site complete with an extraordinary heavy film camera and tripod and I got him inside. At dawn light he began filming. Andrew obtained some superb film and we spent three fascinating days, me going with him to my hide, getting him in and then I'd wander off to sit on the cliffs watching seabirds and rock pipits from my vantage point amongst cushions of pink thrift flowers and white sea campions.

On one occasion pied wagtails flew directly on to the ravens huge stick nest and along the ledge eating the flies attracted by the ravens food of docked lambs tails and a rat. On the third day Andrew said to me how great it would be to have film of the ravens eating from a sheep carcase and could I arrange it. No problem, I told him, racking my brains with no idea how to provide such an item to a pair of ravens, especially as Andrew had only 7 days shooting time. Then it occurred to me. Harold May, the farmer of my schoolboy haunts. I phoned him saying could he let me have a dead sheep so that the BBC Natural History Unit could film ravens eating it. It sounded daft as I said it down the phone with Andrew grinning. When? I was asked. Oh, sort of anytime really, I told him. He told me I was in luck. They had a dead sheep at the farm put aside to go to the Hunt kennels and I could have it as long as I collected it.

No problem, said Andrew, the total enthusiast like myself. Off we went in his car. I had not lifted a dead, rather high smelling sheep before and it was an awful struggle to get it into the back of Andrew's car which had no boot to speak of. Harold stood by watching and grinning as all kinds of mess distributed itself over our clothes and the car seat.

Better open the windows, we were told as in we leapt. It was a hot, sunny, beautiful day, the sheep smell incredible as we raced the nine miles to escape its worse aroma, the stench from the poor animal wafting away behind us. Arriving at the layby above the cliffs we found a number of parked cars with their owners sitting on the stone wall drinking soft drinks, eating ices, just gazing out to sea as normal people do.

Out came the sheep with a rush as I fell backwards and Andrew fell forwards into the car, but it was out. We lifted it to a broken wall area and I dropped into the field watched by the now amazed onlookers as Andrew heaved. Down the slope the carcase rolled to stop against my legs. Over the wall came

Andrew and we lifted the sheep between us with some 400 yards to go, my eyes bulging at the weight of the creature. Andrew was a very strong man. Carting a huge film camera and tripod about, often on his own, is no mean feat as I'd found over the past few days while helping him. Even then it was hard work so it was with a sigh of relief that we eventually rolled our charge over the beach below a cliff 'chimney' I had found, which accessed onto the beach.

We then had to trudge back to get the camera and tripod gear from the car, climbing up onto the road to do so.

"Ah they are film people, that explains it", said one of the onlookers, "they are all barmy".

Barmy or not Andrew and I spent the rest of the day filming, he in the 'chimney', with me on guard. I went to the nearby village at one stage, purchasing pasties, large bars of chocolate and cartons of orange juice. I called to Andrew that food was on its way down, hearing his several yells of pain as each item found its target. But an excellent cameraman and what a superb film the BBC Natural History Unit made of it all.

On another occasion, I think it was the mid 1970s, I was asked to set up some wildlife film scenes for a natural history film being made for young people, or family entertainment where a presenter wanders about the countryside pointing creatures and plants out as he or she tells us about them.

"Can you find me some lizards?" That was my first task on this particular series and despite the decline of the so called common lizard in many areas, I knew where I could find them near my home on warm, sunny days. I said yes, no problem and was told I would receive a copy of the script and instructions and I must adhere strictly to those when the cameraman arrived. I was somewhat puzzled as I wasn't to be in the film but all was soon to be revealed.

The script and instructions duly arrived and under lizards it said that they must be filmed moving from left to right, not in any other direction! New to the game I was more puzzled than ever until the cameraman said when asked, "Ah that's because you and I will go film the lizards today. The presenter wont be down for two or three weeks, until we've finished filming.

"What's the good of that?" says I in my naivity of such matters.

"Well, she'll come down with a different crew and the Director on a day of similar weather. They'll go to the locations you find us and she'll stand or walk and point, 'left to right' or whatever other instructions you are given and the film of that will be edited in with our stuff, and Bob's your uncle".

"So she wont actually see the wildlife then." I said.

"No, no need. Couldn't waste their time like that", he grinned.

"So, get the instructions exactly right and it will all work out smoothly".

We found and filmed lizards, me catching some and releasing them to run across the terrain in the right direction and all went well. For the same series a barn owl and kestrel were brought in and filmed in flight, hand reared birds of course, beautiful to watch and I took some colour transparencies of those. Two years later the lot were taken from our car when I left it to photograph shelduck on a river for a few minutes on the way to give a talk.

The next task in the same series was quite difficult. "Fix it so that we can film a grey heron catching fish in a tidal creek on Tuesday next, around midday".

I may have sounded a bit incredulous when I exclaimed, "What?!"

"Oh don't worry about the heron, we'll bring one. Just make sure there is a creek with live fish in it. Can you do that?"

I was going to say something about ebbing and flowing tides but the Director was a very good naturalist and would know about such things.

"No problem", I answered, "but I may need to spend a few pounds".

"Just do the job and send me the bill. As long as you are there with a tidal creek full of water and fish at 12 noon on Tuesday".

I agreed. After all this was fascinating work and where there's a will and all that.

I checked the tide tables and as I thought, the tide would be out at that time but in any case, there had to be fish to catch. I went down to the river near my home where there are saltings creeks galore and eventually found a couple of ideal locations suiting my plans. I then ordered two sheets of chipboard 8ft by 4ft which were to be delivered on the Tuesday morning to my home. As readers may have guessed, my simple plan was to jam the chipboard into position once the tide was in and that would, I hoped, hold the water in the creek long enough for the filming to be done. On the Monday night I went to the river and I could not believe my luck when I actually waylaid three large eels in a creek, caught them and plonked them in a bucket which I took home. I was so happy at this success I did not mind one bit that I was mud ridden. I'd achieved what I thought was impossible, the gods were smiling upon me.

Tuesday morning. The friend who was going to help me carry the boards couldn't make it after all. They were heavy. I had to walk via a woodland path, then along the path by the saltings, across the saltings to the creek mouths and somehow insert the boards while the tide was in the creek. On my own. Luckily I was a very strong person and used to lifting heavy weights. I grabbed the first board and off I went, out of the garden down through the woods, determined not to let the side down. It was hot and windy but I made good progress until I reached the open river bank to find the wind and an 8ft X 4ft sheet of chipboard didn't get along too well. I must have pirouetted completely about 20 times en route to the creek mouth but I made it. The tide was virtually still, that time when the flow has ceased and the ebb was thinking about doing its job of emptying the great river once more. I swung the sheet of chipboard across, the wind now my friend, taking the sheet perfectly into position as I jammed it into place down into the water and mud. To my delight and some surprise it slotted exactly as I had wanted. I looked back along the mile of pathway and woods knowing I had to do the journey all over again. The second sheet felt a ton heavier but it was only 10am and I knew it would fit if the first one had. I'd chosen two sheets afraid that one would not hold but as I swung the second sheet into place, gasping for breath, it lodged perfectly against its companion. Beavers could not have done a better job of damming and I sat catching my breath for a while.

The fish! They were at home in the large metal bucket of water. I struggled to my feet and walked home. There was no vehicular access to the river in those days though lorries can get close today. I got indoors and decided to spruce up and change from muddy gear, and have a good strong cup of tea before going back with the fish.

A large bucket of water is very heavy. Though Science would disagree it gets heavier by the minute when carried a mile in rough terrain. But by 12 noon when the film people arrived there was a creek full of water, the sediment had more or less cleared, and there were eels and some flounders moving about.

"Brilliant!", said the Director, beaming.

"No problem", I said, beaming in return. With arms and back aching considerably I watched the heron do its stuff. It caught one of the flounders.

The Director and crew departed. As he left he called out, "can you sort out the chipboard, get rid of it, I'll phone you later, in a day or so".

So, I waited a while then with much more difficulty than when I inserted the chipboard sheets, I eventually dragged them out onto the bank and rested them against a factory boundary fence. I then decided to ask someone I knew with a pick-up truck, to fetch them for me if I got them to the road. This was agreed for that evening. I went home and cleaned up again. That evening I went to the river to carry the boards to the pick up point and they were gone, two large sheets of chipboard a useful commodity to someone no doubt and there were several house boats along the river. I phoned in with the bad news and was told not to worry about it, everyone was well pleased with the ease with which I'd accomplished the task. If only they had known how easy it hadn't been.

Once when asked to find a peregrine falcon site and an easily filmable seabird colony I found the latter with ease at a time when razorbills, guillemots, fulmars, cormorants, oystercatchers and gulls were all nesting. I then went off to find the more elusive falcons, having a Schedule One Licence to do so.

Finding the peregrines was easy enough and I could see roughly where the nest site must be below me on the cliffs. I strolled off down across the grass sward on a beautifully sunny day to where a very narrow, rugged path appeared easy to follow. It was in the exact direction towards where I knew the falcons would be.

As I climbed ever down and along the path I found it became about a foot wide and the cliff was now sheer. Thus I found myself edging along it, my body facing inwards, arms akimbo as I made my way onwards ever hoping the path might suddenly widen. My binocular was hung now down my back, my head facing the way I was going could not turn so narrow was the way. I glanced down then quickly away from the sheer drop below, one look at the rocks and waves reminding me I couldn't swim, or fly come to that.

I turned a corner, hearing the high pitched, angry 'kee-kee' sound of an adult peregrine above my head, and there was another perched at a nest site with three young.

There was no ledge situation near or above the birds. I felt a bit odd about it all and looked down. There was no ledge beyond my feet either. I went very cold, in fact I do even now sometimes when I recall that day. I could not turn around, not even my head to look back the way I'd come. I began to inch my way backwards, unable to see where to go, where to put my hands to grip crevices and of course unable to see where I was putting my feet. It took me an hour to get back to safe ground, one of the more frightening experiences of my life, and it felt like a year. When I eventually climbed back up onto the level grass above the cliffs I sat down and began to shake. It was some time before I recovered my composure enough to go back to the car.

I never did tell anyone of the peregrine site but did watch the whole family fly successfully some weeks later. The film crew had learned of an ' easy' site in Ireland and did their filming there. But I have digressed for too long. Back to the nests of birds and observations of other wildlife....

11

Of Water Rails and Wagtails

More by accident than design I discovered a water rail nesting situation one summer. I was more likely to have found it than anyone else I suppose because I regularly revisited old haunts from my school days and would thus don rubber boots and walk the waterways actually in the water rather than along the banks, just as I used to do. I did this just twice a year, once upstream, once downstream. A lot of the waterway ran beneath what could only be called a green tunnel of trees so anyone wandering along its route would rarely be noticed. I walk it very slowly, with great care, sometimes taking the whole day, watching, trying to miss nothing.

Seeing a water rail slip away from a nest, to swim along the leat I was exploring, and disappear into vegetation. I sat in the bushes growing from wet ground and waited. The bird came back onto her eggs which I'd already confirmed were in the nest, and settled down. I waited on and saw the other adult about, a fine sight, and over the course of a few days I recorded the situation on a British Trust for Ornithology Nest Record card, one of many I sent in that year. The nesting was successful, the young hatching, looking like balls of black cotton wool on legs. Apart from my own pleasure at seeing the water rails around and about the nest for several days, and being able to record it for the Atlas of Breeding Birds Survey I was helping with, I placed no particular significance in the discovery, no more than I did for, say, sparrowhawks, lapwing or others considered less common back then in the 1970s.

But eventually, when the Atlas was published, to my surprise I had recorded the first breeding success for water rails in Devon for some 40 years! And did not know it. To me, finding a bird nesting was a joy whatever the species and I had not realised just how rare Rallus aquaticus was as a breeding species. Indeed I doubt it was quite as rare as suggested for the water rail is a most secretive bird, particularly when it has eggs and young, and it does prefer secluded habitats so may well have been overlooked many times over the years.

So there is was. A bit of birdwatching history. I've found a number of water rail nesting situations since, right up to the present day.

Yellow Wagtails

The yellow wagtails nest I kept watch on was in a hollow against a grassy bank adjoining a wood edge and flat to the ground. The site was fairly open but with partial shelter from nettles and ferns. The nest was solitary and I was surprised to find it, as I thought, some distance from water but I later discovered a small natural pond fed by springs nearby. Using my binocular from a tree vantage point I counted five eggs when the female was off the nest, noticing they were quite like the eggs of the less brightly coloured grey wagtail.

For almost two weeks the female incubated the eggs, often running off when a particular vixen moved across the field of an evening and usually hovering over the nest before landing on her return. Once or twice as I arrived on site the male called the female off and then when she returned she'd often hover elsewhere than at the nest before finally settling on it. Interestingly she was not called off when the fox was about, as if the male felt humans were the greater danger. At no time did a passing fox bother the incubating bird at all.

Once hatched the two adults set about the task of feeding them, the golden glow of evening light seeming to set the whole scene and the yellow birds alight at times, a stunningly beautiful sight as they flitted about finding food for the young and themselves. Fledging took 13 days. I felt this was a late nest as it was July when I happened on the situation. Yellow wagtails often raise two broods in a year so it was possibly the second brood though I saw no others of the species in the vicinity. With the spring being wet it is quite likely the wagtails did not have an early brood of course.

Grey Wagtails

One summer, 1974 as I recall, I was observing grey wagtails, dippers and moorhens all nesting along a waterway when the weather changed dramatically from sunshine to rain, heavy rain over several days. When I went back to the valley on the first fine day the fields, some old water meadows, were flooded, the stream running through the valley up to the level of the plank bridge spanning two of the fields.

I found the grey wagtails nest washed away completely and with sinking heart went further upstream to where the dippers were nesting. Their nest had survived. Even now it was just above the rushing water surface but intact. Moreover, to my absolute surprise and delight the two grey wagtails were busy feeding the young dippers, helping the two adult dippers with the task of parenthood, all four birds dashing to and fro with food for the four young.

It was a very moving moment, one I shall never forget. I must have made the discovery about mid way through the fledging period as I was able to revisit over the nest 10 or 12 days until the young left the nest and dippers usually fledge from 19-25 days.

As for the moorhens they had built their nest up much higher than I remembered it, which is fairly typical in rainy times. They brought off 6 young successfully.

12

Raptors

I monitored many birds of prey nests over the years, buzzard, sparrowhawk, kestrel, hobby and merlin mostly, and again had to have a Schedule One Licence for sparrowhawk, merlin and hobby as all at that time were in need of special protection due to low numbers. Today that status has been removed for sparrowhawk as it has recovered quite well.

My merlin and hobby observations attracted the attention of the British Trust for Ornithology, then at Tring in Hertfordshire, as I was submitting detailed Nest Record Cards to them. Before long I was corresponding with the great Desmond Nethersole-Thompson, and Dr Dieter Fiucynski, the latter in Berlin and both studying these two falcons, Desmond in Scotland of course.

These were fascinating days. I was inspired to work harder on my monitoring, spending hundreds of hours in the field evenings, weekends, even early mornings before going to work.

I saw many clashes between green woodpeckers and hobbies, the latter quite bold in defence of eggs and young. They nested usually in former nests of crows, often very high up for, unlike hawks, falcons do not build their own nests. The hobbies would chase and catch dragonflies, often hunting over a nearby lake or the river running through the valley, and many is the time they would chase down insect hunting house martins.

I watched 'my' merlins on Exmoor mostly, occasionally on Dartmoor, and once or twice in the Quantocks where we also watched nightjars quite a lot. To my mind merlins are very special and I found I had an odd sort of rapport with them. After several visits to one particular site in an Exmoor coombe the cock merlin suddenly stopped his warnings when I arrived and would accompany me to my usual observation spot amongst some rocky outcrops, the merlin flitting from one rock to another close by me. I used to sit on the opposite coombe side to the merlin's nest, this one on the ground amongst heather, and watch the female, then the other bird life and dragonflies zooming up and down nearby.

One morning I arrived early to find no sign of life. After waiting awhile I slowly and carefully climbed the steep slope to the nest to find the female sitting close. She looked up at me and I'll never forget her eyes or the feeling of trust between us which was immensely powerful. I did not imagine it, the bond was there. I knelt and stroked her head and she closed her eyes as I did so, remaining on the nest in the 'L' shaped rock shelter. It was an overwhelming experience. I moved away across the coombe side, hearing the cock merlin call a rapid, "kee, kee, kee" as he flew into view from somewhere along the coombe. A while later he caught a small bird and I decided to leave them to their privacy in this wonderful place and do some birdwatching elsewhere.

I watched that nest and others through to successful hatching, some in former crows nests in rowan and hawthorn trees and one or two other ground nests, as over the years I concentrated largely on observing birds of prey, the raptors as they are known.

Sparrowhawks

A wonderful little hawk, in serious decline from pesticide poison a few decades ago but now recovering though not back to numbers of old. Afforestation has helped the sparrowhawk where nesting is concerned, a much needed if inadvertent boost as so much broadleaved woodland has been felled in recent years, much depleting habitat for many wildlife species.

I monitored many sparrowhawk nests since the 60s as part of a serious study I made of raptors, discovering what excellent parents the adults make during the breeding season and beyond.

At one woodland site I found two occupied sparrowhawk

nests in close proximity, measured at no more than 30 yards apart in two separate trees. This was not a case of an adult male with two mates but of two completely separate pairs, both breeding and with eggs and eventually, young to feed.

I informed the BTO on Nest Record Cards and some excitement ensued as this was the second closest two nests of sparrowhawks ever recorded, the closest pairs being only 22 yards apart in a forest in Dumfreisshire, Scotland. Both of these records are now in the 'Handbook of the British Birds of Europe, the Middle East & North Africa", Vol 2 of this nine volume work.

It was a fascinating summer observing the hawks, especially as the two males would leave the nests area and fly in opposite directions to hunt as if they had agreed to share the woods and valley between them with no clashes. When the young were being fledged the whole scene was quite amazing, the constant toing and froing of the four adults, and eventually the young learning to fly and so on. Quite an experience and a great learning time for me. In all the hours I watched the site I did not once see a clash occur between any of the hawks, adults or young. Wonderful birds.

Buzzards

The 'eagle' of the Westcountry as some call it, the buzzard is our largest hawk, a fine sight soaring on the thermals, the warm air currents, over many a wooded valley, moorland and coastal area, its mewing cry well known by all who live here.

I have monitored more buzzard's nests than any other raptor species probably, corresponding for a number of years, to compare notes, with the late Colin Tubbs who wrote 'The Buzzard', and did much monitoring in the New Forest.

Of all the many strange and wonderful incidents one that stands out most in my memory is of pulling myself up level with the top of a buzzard's nest to find an adder staring at me. That gave me a jolt, especially at some 30ft up a tree! No doubt I descended that tree much faster than usual. I have seen buzzards flying with snakes hanging in their talons before, and rats and rabbits of course, and have seen a buzzard snatch a rabbit from under the jaws of a fox as the two were both hunting the same prey.

Buzzards are usually faithful to one area over the course of several years, their young dispersing to find territories of their own at about the autumn or early winter of the year of their birth as it were.

Kestrels

Once our commonest bird of prey but rarer than for some decades though it is difficult to reason why. It may be that kestrels are more prone to pesticides than other raptors as a lot of chemicals are used on the land and they get into the food chains one way or another, even into our own of course.

Like buzzards, kestrels often nest at coastal sites so may be found in small caves using former nests of jackdaws and crows. Being a falcon, the kestrel does not build a nest but adapts those of other species.

I have had kestrels as sick or injured birds over the years, along with pretty well all the bird species one could imagine, even to a marsh harrier one year. On one occasion I was called to a cottage near the village of Bratton Fleming in Devon where a kestrel had dropped into a chimney. The woman, who lived in the cottage all alone, told me that she was sitting in the dark watching a horror film on TV when suddenly there was a rush of soot and this screaming apparition appeared in the fireplace just feet from her armchair! The kestrel must have been roosting on the chimney I imagine and who was the most scared we can but guess. As it was the bird was unharmed and after a clean up and food it went off next day in fine fettle with a warning from me not to listen to TV down chimneys in future.

Owls

Owls are everyone's favourites. Whether it's their sheer beauty, or the fact they have such expressive faces and are somewhat mysterious creatures of the night I'm not sure but loved they are and rightly so.

When with young to feed and care for woe betide intruders for they are fearsome birds with no fear, attacking anyone who appears likely to be harmful to their eggs or nestlings. Quite right too of course. We are the same.

Readers will recall the incident involving Eric Hosking the well known bird photographer who actually lost an eye to a tawny owl attack in this manner, the bird protecting its nest site.

I was checking an area for barn owls with a friend and we'd just seen one fly from an old barn way out on the marshes so I said I'd go and see if there were any pellets we could take to examine. All was silent in the barn so I reached above my head, grasping the edge of the loft to haul myself up and suddenly a barn owl was upon me, raking the skin from the backs of my hands and taking my old country hat from my head. I let go and dropped. We got out of there fast, staying in a nearby hedgerow to watch the owls back. My own fault of course and I'm pleased to say the young barn owls fledged successfully from the site several weeks later.

I recounted an incident with an oiled tawny owl earlier in the book, which again shows the amazing power and grip of the talons of owls and birds of prey. We have little owls about, too, the ones I observed in a nest situation for my project being in a long disused mine shaft. I've also found nesting little owls in sheds, hollow trees and rabbit burrows, delightful little birds with their serious 'frown' appearance and interesting behaviour. Not so difficult to observe either as they are often about by day.

In the late 1950s I found short eared owls nesting in North Devon whilst long eared owls bred in two or three places right up until very recent times, once in an old sunken lane, but usually in conifer plantations I find. Both species tend to be wintering birds here in the main and breeding is uncommon indeed.

13

Mustelids & Other Wild Animals

Otters, badgers, stoats, weasels and mink all come under the Mustela Family heading so to speak, all having musky scent glands close by their anus, something one discovers from books or from handling some of the creatures.

Living where I do I've grown up seeing all of the above countless times, the mink appearing in the wild since the 1950s, along with myxomatosis in rabbits and deaths by pesticides of many birds and other animals. The mink were from fur farms, escapes and releases, and they soon spread across country and bred. Thus was born the feral mink in the UK and here in the Westcountry they became quite common, doing much damage to other wildlife, particularly along and close to waterways. Most are a dark chocolate brown colour though some were silver, some black and colours in between for they were bred for furs for the fashion trade. They are undoubtedly attractive animals but we did not need another top predator in the food chain especially with the declines in other wildlife species, which are not really new and have been occurring for three or four decades without much publicity until recently, though the reality of that is down to modern farming methods and not due to predators.

No one knew much about mink in the wild other than what they ate but as they are often about by day and about the size of a ferret we soon got to know them and their ways.

My first real encounter was on a fresh water marsh where two of us had been watching reed and sedge warblers which I was attempting unsuccessfully to photograph amongst the reeds. My companion suddenly pointed out a mink well in amongst some alders and I thought what a fine photo or two it would make. We went carefully into the marsh and lo and behold the mink ran up a leaning willow tree trunk to perch amongst its branches. Better than ever I thought and camera ready, I went up the tree after it.

Dearie me! What a wild little animal it turned out to be. Instead of posing for a photo, which would have done neither of us any harm, it bared its fangs in a most ferocious manner and charged. Well, as with the barn owl on a previous occasion, the rule is if an animal doesn't want you in its territory, the wise accept any gesture that hints at bloody confrontation as a time to withdraw. We withdrew and last saw the mink high tailing it across the marshes. I did find a mink lair in the roots of a hollow tree, discovering a cache of bird's wings, feathers and legs and feet of moorhens, wagtails, coot and scores of starlings. Obviously this particular mink had discovered a winter reed bed starling roost was a good place to be for many thousands flew in to form huge clouds of birds each night before sunset, both mink and sparrowhawk availing themselves of a regular supper, and possibly breakfast here.

Mink have now 'evened out' and are not so abundant these days, many having been trapped and killed as part of a MAFF (Now DEFRA) eradication project. I believe they were 'notifiable' animals at one time and they may still be so. It is a fine animal and tis sad they were exploited into this situation by humans.

Otters are wonderful to watch and I urge anyone to see an otter in the wild just once in a lifetime. Otter hunting was banned in the late 1970s, the animal an endangered species in need of special protection.

I helped the Vincent Wildlife Trust set up the first Otter Havens in North Devon thanks to farmers and other landowners with riparian ownerships. Several imitation otter holts were also built at likely places along rivers, streams and at reservoirs. I did 12 years of Haven monitoring until the VWT handed them over to the Royal Society for Nature Conservation. I was allowed to retain 8 of the Havens I regularly monitored, they becoming Wildlife Havens, the idea the basis of the now well known Western Morning News Wildlife Havens, begun in February 1999 to mark the New Millennium. As I write, that project is now at 6,200 acres and still going strong. Thanks to otters, shall we say, so many other species have been helped along with thousands of acres of habitat.

The stories of large numbers of weasels, and of stoats, wandering the countryside in packs are legend, and quite true. I have seen such packs on several occasions, undoubtedly family groups, or two or more families and they are often associated with hard times in terms of low food availability. Hunting together, rather as lions do on the plains of Africa, may well mean the obtaining of more or larger prey. Luck plays a great part in such sightings whilst it is also very true that the more one is out and about nature watching, the more one is likely to see. Being in the right place at the right time is a happy mix of getting out of doors and some good luck.

Badgers

I shudder to think how many hours I've spent observing badgers, mostly at night and what superb animals they are. Again, I could write a book just about badgers but of the many incidents that stand out in my mind over several decades, even moreso than watching cubs romping on moonlit nights, one always moves me to tears when it comes to mind.

For the third time in many years of night watching for wildlife I have witnessed an incident that seems to transcend others and leaves me deeply moved. I had been quietly watching three or four badgers on the cleave slope for about three-quarters of an hour when they all turned to face the sett, standing stock still. Another badger moved onto the hillside, a bit odd looking until we realised it was being pushed from the sett entrance by another. The first badger was dead. Its mate, I guessed it was its mate, nudged it onto the slope until it rolled down for some thirty to forty feet to rest against the bramble brake there.

It was difficult to tell boar from sow in the shadows of the moonlit field but the bereaved badger was a female, I thought. For over twenty minutes she brought old bedding out onto the hillside, then took it down to her mate's side. She pulled him a little further under the cover of brambles, then covered him completely with the bedding, watched all the time by the other badgers, and me. Next she moved earth and stones from the hedgebank until there was nought to be seen but a burial mound, a barrow of you like. She stood beside the grave for a while, head bowed. Then she turned and moved off into the darkness of the woods. Each of the watching badgers went to the graveside, then followed her into the woods.

It is impossible to write more about it. It was how it was. I could find no words then and went our way. A day or two later I put more stones and earth upon the little grave.

Fascinating animals with a special place in my heart. I pray they will always be about, that the awful culling of badgers is very soon a thing of the past and that they receive our unlimited respect and affection into the future. We owe it to them.

Foxes
Like many other animals, and some plants come to that, foxes are loved by some, ignored by others and maligned by a few. Often the dislike of foxes and other species of fauna and flora is an inherited thing, often without sound basis yet others might say there is no sound basis for loving a fox. Me, I have a love for most living things, probably all if I look at it from the viewpoint that life is sweet for the liver of that life in the main. My philosophy is I am not here to kill any living thing beyond needs for food and that goes for both animals and plants. It is a view untaught, one I reached for myself and I wont back down on it.

I have made a special study of several mammal species including the fox over many years so I feel I know the animal extremely well. I also realise from these studies which, by the way, are ongoing, that foxes and other creatures are very much individuals just as much as people are, even though we tend to generalise when it comes to behaviour, always a mistake I must firmly say. And, as well as being individuals from day one, behaviour in a wild animal changes with the aging process, perhaps more markedly than with ourselves who tend to follow laid down results, called 'being civilised.'

It would be impossible to cover the ways of a fox within the limited scope of this book so I have written a life story, 'Old Red'. It tells the story of a Devon dog fox from early cubhood to his mating with a vixen born some five or six miles from his birthplace. Each incident is factual, observed with my own eyes though of course, not all of one single fox, but many scores of observations built into one life story. A lovely animal deserving our respect and better understanding.

14

Fun in the Woods & Elsewhere

There are two ways in which I look at photography for my work. The shots I take for the regular columns I write for the regions best daily, The Western Morning News, and for magazines and such must be genuine. However, if I am putting together a colour slide illustrated talk I may sometimes do a 'sandwhich' job by putting two slides, or transparencies as they are called, together for effect. For example a shot of a gull soaring against a plain blue sky, framed with a shot of a sunset, draws more oohs and aahs at talks. I learned this trick in the 1970s when the late Dr Colin Bibby an RSPB Research Biologist stayed with me for a few days and whilst here, gave a fine talk to our members group. One of his slides, his final one of the evening, showed a peregrine in silhouette stooping out of a wonderful sunset with the scenery also in sharp focus. How did you get that shot, was my question to him to him on the way home and so I learned of blending two transparencies to produce one stunning shot.

Anyway four or five of us went to my private wildlife sanctuary one day to do some photography for talks so for a bit of fun I took with me a favourite stuffed woodcock taxidermied in the 'sitting position' of a bird resting up.

We had taken a picnic and R, one of the company, who fixes onto food like a magnet was too busy chewing to observe what I was doing. I casually wandered down the wood slope, depositing the woodcock just in under some brambles and surrounded it with leaves. It looked very authentic. Lunch over I remarked, "goodness look at that", pointing to the bird, "What a photo that would make".

R immediately bade us all stay still, saying he would show us what a skilful stalker he was. With this particular bird I had no doubts about his stalking ability but I found it difficult to refrain from chuckling. R very slowly stood up, removing his camera from his bag of tricks and even more slowly he made a very wide detour off amongst the trees. Several minutes later he appeared 'commando style' holding said camera as he crawled supported by his elbows from the shrubs to slowly and painstakingly make his way towards his quarry.

"But isn't that your woodcock from home?" Endymion asked me, to which I replied "Ssh!" It was all I could say for I was having desperate troubles preventing myself from calling out to him.

On R went, through some nettles which caused a momentary niggle of annoyance to cross his face and then he was within six feet of the woodcock. He will now realise the bird isn't real I thought, watching now with my binocular as were the others all racked with silent glee. But no, R was lying now fully stretched and triumphant. The woodcock's eyes gleamed as R pressed the shutter. 'Click, click, click' went the motor drive and R moved closer still taking more shots. He then backed away, still on hands and knees, to beckon me down for my turn. Camera in hand I walked casually down the slope to the bird, bent down pulling it out into the sunlight as I said I thought I'd get a shot in better light.

R was very quiet for a moment or two, then, "You b-idiot Beer", he roared, the use of my surname leaving no doubt in our minds that he was a tad miffed. It was three or four days before he'd look me in the eye again. Even now, years later I feel he may try to think up a return practical joke. Perhaps it was he who had two of us travel thirty miles to an Exmoor location to see "the Exmoor Beast" that has been on the prowl for some years now. The call was from a call box which I rang back to verify it was not a hoax call. The caller answered, said he would wait and there was no one there when we arrived!

There was a lot of hoaxing going on over the years from the early 1980s when the big-cats, the pumas and black leopards, first blazed across newspapers, radio and TV. Cardboard cutouts were photographed and in the papers. As I was quite involved in the investigations I was hoaxed several times, one woman calling Radio Devon with a message from me that I knew nothing about; another actually phoning me purporting to be from a Society I was giving a talk to that week, and cancelling the talk as there was some "mix-up with dates". So I cancelled the room and didn't turn up. And the society members did! Yet another phone call, supposedly from Bideford Library, asked me to mount a wildlife exhibition of my stuffed animals in the library. Endymion, who was free of work that week, piled a box with necessary items and caught a bus the nine miles to Bideford only to be told by the librarian they hadn't phoned us! Hoaxers all. A bit of fun is fine, a practical joke always good for a chuckle, but travelling for miles with such a load is not so amusing, and back again of course.

As I say, a bit of fun yes. I had a call to visit a shop in town to collect a prize I'd won. I said I could not recall entering any competition. The caller said good customers names had been put in a box and mine was the name drawn. As I frequented the shop I went into town to find they had no competition running. Another told me I had won an award for conservation work, quite a hefty prize being involved. The award name was genuine and had to do with my work. The caller said I was to choose my own prize, pay for it and hold the receipt pending the award evening. I said I had not entered for any awards. No, but you have been nominated by someone else and we must not say who as yet as it isn't public knowledge, blah, blah, I was told.

I ordered an item which was not in stock locally and it was found for me. I then did some homework on the award evening as to when it would be and yes, another hoax and some embarrassment on my part. But then, someone had a laugh from it I suppose.

One such that I played myself was on a very rainy day. Occasionally a few of us might meet up of a lunch hour to bird watch by the river for a bit of fresh air. I phoned my acquaintance saying there were several rose coloured swans on the River Yeo but I could not get away to see them. "I'll go, and tell the others", said T. It absolutely poured, cats and dogs weather all that lunch hour. After lunch the intrepid three arrived back at the office soaked to the skin. "No luck", said T "only a few mute swans, all white ones as usual".

"Well haven't you seen white roses?" I asked, the three having fallen for one of the old classics.

I was roughed up with three very sodden raincoats.

15
Those Talks!

There was a time, for several years, that I used to be asked to give talks to W.Is, Mothers Union Groups, and various other organisations in the Westcountry. I also held Courses for the Workers Educational Association at the Community Colleges tutoring evening classes on wildlife and nature conservation.

It was usually good fun, the W.Is always a pleasure, some of their members giving me information which was extremely useful. There was always a cheery cup of tea and a chat and usually a competition to judge and as I did not charge a fee, the petrol expenses were usually offered.

The occasional mess-up was inevitable, times when one had been booked the year before and had the 'flu' or some winter malady by the time the talk was due. It was impossible to look ahead of course but I almost always found someone else to fill in for me.

On three occasions I arrived to find double bookings had been made and someone else was also setting up to talk. Once I'd travelled 30 miles on a bitterly cold night and the Secretary said sorry but a former secretary had gotten it wrong. There was nothing one could do but go home again.

I tutored a WEA Course of 8 weeks duration at Dolton, a village in the heart of the Torridge River Country. There was a goodly sized crowd but from the first few minutes of the first evening a woman was determined to 'join in'. That wasn't so bad as I always invited a 'two-way' evening, enjoying the rapport of such occasions. However, this elegant, elderly lady who wore large, wide brimmed hats and was obviously well educated and of considerable knowledge had shot just about everything in her day, and eaten it. Each time I put up a colour transparency slide to discuss a bird she'd call out, "I've shot those, and eaten that", and so on. Curlew, swan, wildfowl, the eggs of moorhens and hams of badgers, she had with her family feasted on most creatures of the countryside it seemed and proceeded to tell me so with a relish, even to how some were cooked. It was indeed educational and I wondered if there was any wildlife left in the area at all.

I had audiences of 250 or more people at maximum and as low as one! This latter audience was at a community college of all places and the organiser had omitted to advertise the talk that had long been booked by him. When I arrived with my projector and screen he had found this lone 'audience' when it would have been better to have called it a day. I of course suggested surely he didn't want to sit through a talk on his own but the fellow said he would actually like to hear it. So, with my selection of slides I gave my 75 minute talk to this very silent gentleman who's been 'roped in' by the Adult Tutor Organiser and when I finished and had turned to put the lights on he'd gone and all I saw was a swinging door and empty room.

I did have a nil audience at our local museum. Again posters had been forgotten so no one knew. I set up the equipment in readiness when the curator told me what had happened, so I loaded the car again and went home.

Winter nights could be dreadful. At one W.I hall it was so very cold everyone sat in their coats visibly shivering as I delivered my talk with chattering teeth. It was mass hypothermia and I felt ill for days afterwards. On another occasion my projector suddenly went off and I cursed thinking the bulb had failed. I called out my apologies in the dark and stumbled to the back of the hall to turn on the lights. Nothing happened. Then a small voice said, "Oh dear, has anybody got a shilling for the meter?"

Fortune smiled. I had the only shilling in the crowd so with the help of the secretary whose red face almost glowed in the dark I eventually found the electric meter, restored the lighting and rushed through my talk in case the lights went out again.

One day on my way to Minehead in Somerset, from

Barnstaple, we were crossing the moor when our Morris 1000, a most reliable car which never let me down, started to heat up and blow steam. I'd forgotten to check the water and there was just the one house in sight. It was a dark, winter's night and I trudged to the house and knocked on the door. The lights went out, then a light upstairs came on an a woman peered from a window.

"What do you want?", she enquired in a peeved tone of voice.

"Could I have some water please?" I asked and explained the predicament.

"No you cannot. How do I know who you are?" She replied.

I told her who I was and said I was on my way to Minehead to talk to the Exmoor Natural History Society there. Still she refused, telling me to go away. I told her there were milk bottles on the step, could I just fill those with water, sort out my problem and go. No, she told me, but there is a garage two miles down the road so go there. Bidding her goodnight off I went into the darkness, eventually finding the garage which was open, the fellow sending his son back with me by car and I was shortly on my way again. The Minehead evening was packed to capacity, people standing at the back and along the sides of the very large room. My talk was well received, refreshments were excellent and the moorland incident soon forgotten. Hours later when we passed the lone house on our return journey one could somehow understand the woman's fears, even though I'd arrived smartly dressed, with a vehicle steaming away at the end of her drive.

As I have said, the vast majority of talks were fun to do. At one I met a gentleman who became a good friend for a few years before he moved away. I had been telephoned by the WEA to ask if I could 'rescue' a Course that had started at Bideford based on wildlife. The WEA Organiser told me the tutor taking the course had reached week three and there were complaints from the course members. It turned out the tutor, booked to fill 7pm to 9pm evenings, ran out of thoughts by 8pm and told the audience, and this was a paid for course, to "talk amongst themselves" for the second hour! I took my slides to week 4 to be faced by stony silence, the audience obviously in a mood after three weeks of the other situation. After a while I was being asked questions about North Devon's bird and other wildlife and suddenly everything clicked. The course went very well, I making sure I filled each minute, with fresh colour slides each week and then offering a wildlife walk as an extra. Everyone came, some bringing wives or husbands and we had a great time.

It was here I met B, a huge man. I am 6ft 2ins tall and lean. He was my height and about as broad as he was long and jolly with it. He wanted to become a "real birdwatcher" he said, and to "know all the birds".

We soon forged a friendship, meeting up at various bird watching sites as I suggested and B became very keen. He was a single man, living with his mother and had moved down from the Midlands as a key worker for a large company making electrical components which went all over the world, and still do.

On one occasion a Sacred Ibis visited North Devon, staying with us for two or three years in fact before it was shot in error by a wildfowler. On one winters day we went in search for the bird at Braunton Marshes, soon finding it and taking photos.

I offered to take B out across the marsh to look for other wintering birds on the ponds often filled with coot, teal and other species. He readily agreed so I told him to keep close to me and never to walk on the lime green areas, which I carefully pointed out. He grinned and said he was O.K and could see where he was going. Off we went, me in the lead when suddenly I heard his cry for help. He had taken a short-cut across the 'lime green patches' I'd told him to avoid and was right up to his knees in the quagmire, looking somewhat crest fallen. B was around 17 stone. There was no way an ordinary mortal could go into the morass, keep from sinking and lift him free at the same time.

I told him to do as I said this time and he nodded. I told him to fall forward then inch his way toward the nearest dry ground, which I pointed out to him, telling him to swing his camera and binocular around to his back. B did as I bid him, mud going up to his elbows as he turned dark grey with oozing mud, wallowing like a hippo. Inch by inch he dragged himself forward until I could grab a wrist without losing my own footing and then with a mighty effort on both our parts he was on the solid ground beside me.

"Look at my new watch", he said with a wail, though in fact it could not really be seen beneath the mud already caking on most of his large frame.

"You've lost your boots", I told him. "They've been sucked off".

"I've been very lucky I reckon", B said. "But it all looked so green and solid".

We eventually made it back to the car, lessons learned. Such is life.

I learned a lesson of my own at these same marshes one summer. I'd put up my portable hide which was basically four poles, a well made camouflage material hide with slits for windows and a camera tunnel, and four guy-ropes which anchored with metal skewers. They were excellent hides and I'd spent fascinating hours in mine watching and photographing wildlife whilst sitting on a fishing stool inside.

On this particular day I'd just set up on a bank overlooking the marsh ponds, actually a 'trapped' former meander of the river which had been diverted as part of a land reclamation exercise in the 1800s. Now the pools were home to a wealth of wildlife including one or two rarities, freshwater marshes themselves being a rarity in this day and age, with so much land drainage.

My objective was to photograph a pair of little grebes which I knew were breeding deep in the reeds across a stretch of water, my fervent hope being that they would come out into the open to pose on the mirror-like water for me. Whatever else came would be a bonus, so I sat happily watching sedge warblers about their business and listening to the early morning marsh sounds.

Suddenly the hide seemed to move on one side as well as behind me. I went to look out of the small window on that side when I felt a great weight moving and heard the snapping of one of my hide poles. Instinctively I hurriedly pulled the two poles beside me, uprooting them and lifting the hide material I threw myself outside to find myself amongst the feet of curious young cattle. I sprang to my feet to see one of these still attempting to scratch himself using the hide to lean on. It was a momentary fright but one I have never forgotten. Shooing the livestock away I rescued the hide and left the area. Curious cattle and people in portable hides do not mix.

The hide disappeared one day from where I'd left it on site close to a fox's earth, wanting to photograph the cubs at play. It was on my own private land in a wood so it seemed a safe enough place. The hide had given me years of pleasure and I imagine somewhere in the Westcountry it is still in use.

There are strict rules of course when photographing or watching wildlife, some to do with the law, some we must self impose. Never disturb wildlife or cause a creature stress especially whilst breeding for they are then extremely vulnerable and may desert their homes. Always put the wild creature or plant first.

As to the law some creatures are specially protected and in the case of certain birds for example, a special licence may be required to photograph or disturb them in the breeding season. Your Police Wildlife Crime Officer will tell you about this, or contact the British Trust for Ornithology who are currently at The Nunnery, Thetford, Norfolk, asking for their Licensing Department.

I tutored several courses of eight or more weeks duration for Community College evening classes and used to link the talks with walks, pretty well always good fun and we'd see a lot of wildlife especially on Exmoor or Dartmoor, always the favourite venues.

Serious bird watching was always interspersed with amusing incidents on these, the simple things somehow always the funniest. On a walk from Challacombe to the Longstone Menhir on Exmoor, and down the lovely River Bray to Swincombe Reservoir we'd stop for packed lunches at the edge of a beech wood with redstarts nesting beside us each summer.

On one of these trips the Fairies were in a funny mood. One

fellow had his wife hold two cups as he opened their vacuum flask. His face as he poured and nothing came out was a picture, his wife's references to his catering efficiency quite caustic. Another fellow dropped his very hard boiled egg and we all watched it bounce down over the steep hillside to the marshy ground below with him in hot, very hot, pursuit. The egg plopped into the Bray River which here is very narrow and but a chattering moorland stream. He crawled back up, scarlet, perspiring and panting, eggless and legless.

"That stuff Trevor, that stuff, gasp, that you, gasp, told us about last week, gasp. You know, gasp, it eats insects".

"Oh, sundew. Wonderful, so you've found some. I'll photograph it later." I answered.

"Yes, gasp. Down there at the valley bottom. It, gasp, eats eggs too," he chuckled.

But tiny mishaps do not mar a day. We'd always see ring ouzels and stonechats along with the redstarts, sometimes pied as well as spotted flycatchers, and usually red deer and a fox or two, as well as the wildflowers and butterflies everywhere.

At W.I talks I usually gained as much information as I gave. The W.I ladies are all deeply into the various aspects of their village or area and I learned a great deal of local history, not only because the members were keen on the subject but largely because many of them had been born thereabouts and had hand me down stories and photographs from parents and ancestors.

The big annual Group Meetings were a pleasure, good company, lots of tea and cake and always the excellent Competitions which the guest speaker would judge. A plain and simple man myself I usually chose the pretty but less ornate exhibits which must have puzzled some of the exhibitors who'd produced amazing works which must sometimes have taken hours of work. However, it was always done in high spirits. Great times those.

I well remember a Mother's Union I used to get asked back to talk to, all seeming to love wildlife and countryside talks. We'd end up nattering away until the caretaker started banging about and then the chatting would continue in the car park.

On one occasion, just as I'd introduced the theme of my talk there was much crashing from the upstairs room directly above us. That room had been booked for a five a side football match, hard to compete with noise-wise but I got through my hour and a quarter and was glad of a strong cup of tea afterwards.

Some tips for those considering giving talks. Have your own projector and other equipment if it's an illustrated talk so that you are sure how everything works. Take along an extension lead. Wall points are often in the wrong place to accommodate seating arrangements.

Always carry a spare projector bulb and check that all your colour transparencies are the correct way up. I went to a talk once where over twenty shots were upside-down and though the speaker laughed it off he'd obviously not done his homework. I find that irritating. I always ran mine through beforehand at home, a professional presentation being only right and proper when people take the trouble to leave their homes at night and travel to see and hear a talk, more especially if they have paid admission.

Just occasionally there are the 'snipers' at talks, who appear to attend to find any fault they can, to appear 'clever' for some reason. They are few and far between, though we have one in our area renowned for it at both walks and talks. Give them as good as they dish out early on is the secret and they usually shut up. I noticed this fellow coming in to one of my talks whispering to a crony and grinning around so I called out his name at the beginning and asked if he suffered from insomnia that he had to come to one of my talks to get some sleep. There was a howl of laughter and he sat quietly through the whole evening.

All in all, if your nerves can stand the strain, giving talks can be both interesting and enjoyable for all concerned which is basically all that they should be. I have done hundreds and know my nervousness showed at times, especially in the early days. I still feel it, butterflies a day before sometimes, but I learned to hide it a bit in time. Now I have cut down almost entirely on them, doing just the odd one for a good cause. All over the years I only accepted petrol money and even then only if the venue was over 20 miles distant. Anything less and I literally gave the talks, though some groups wanted to donate to nature conservation. When this occurred I'd put up a nestbox with their title on it somewhere in the wild and tell them what birds used it, or took them all for a summer walk of a weekend to see some of the wildlife we'd talked about.

Photographing wildlife becomes easier these days due to camera technology of course, to 'fill a frame' being easier at a distance now with all the wonderful lenses available. Nonetheless to obtain good pictures of breeding birds still requires skill and patience, luck, and most importantly the knowing that we must never put the picture first but always the subject.

I built a hide one wet summer and blackbirds nested in it almost immediately. I'd built it looking down into bluebell woods to a foxes earth with cubs and never did get to use it that critical four or five weeks. From the time the hen blackbird sat to lay her clutch, and the time the nestlings fledged I had to stay away from the hide site to avoid disturbing them.

I built a permanent hide of rustic timber which 'hides' well in our Sanctuary woodland. Deer come to within yards and watching birds is a joy at close range. However, the hide is nested in almost every year by blackbird, robin or wood pigeon so there are times when we have to avoid 'their' house in the woods. Stock doves raised two young in the hide one summer but have not continued the practice.

Hides are useful and there are portable ones which are excellent and made of camouflage materials. These usually have window apertures, camera tunnels and all the necessary guy ropes, pegs and pockets. I suggest a folding type 'fishing seat' of canvas should be part of ones equipment and the best tip of all, always carry a black bin liner or two. There's a lot of wet grass about and they make for comfortable 'ground sheets' for sitting on. But, do not leave them or any other rubbish in the countryside. Not only is it a downright eyesore, it kills wildlife. Laziness isn't worth a cuss, and has no part in the ways of a good naturalist.

Camouflage colours to ones clothing is important. Wearing white or pale colours advertises our presence and ruins many a good opportunity for close observation of wildlife. This applies to photography. In the town close by the area I live in there is an excellent Army & Navy Surplus Store with a mass of clothing of the right colours suitable for our varied seasons, as well as other useful equipment. Our Army, Navy and Air Force are well equipped and are not supplied with poor gear. Use it is my advice.

I have never been a 'twitcher', one of those who pursue sightings of rare and uncommon species all over the UK and elsewhere. It tends to be a bird related thing for I have not heard of mammal or wildflower twitchers though no doubt they exist. That isn't to say I am against 'twitching' in principle. As long as it is carried out with the best interests of the birds in mind and there is no disturbance, say, of a vagrant who may well be feeling forlorn and hungry, that's fine. But it isn't for me.

For me there is an excitement in every trip out. There remains an anticipation that has not diminished from boyhood days and I count myself very fortunate in that respect. True I don't climb trees like I used to, I take life at a more sedate pace shall we say, but I feel a thrill at seeing rarities when they come my way as I pursue the more ordinary yet no less beautiful animals and plants each day.

In this last year or so I have met with a golden oriole, hoopoes, yellow wagtails and shrikes, ring-billed gulls, long billed dowitcher, a Richard's pipit and yellow browed warbler, all birds to stir twitchers into action. In a marsh recently a bittern and an otter were present with water rails, all near my home so what more could one wish for.

These and many more I met on my usual jaunts, usually with my collies, Shepherd, Bracken, and now, Willow. We've covered some miles together and I owe them a great deal, for a dog gets you out and about in all weathers at times when you might otherwise avoid getting cold and soaked. Quite often that has led to exciting finds, especially in estuarine habitats in winter when so many waders and wildfowl are about.

I once climbed over a wire fence to find something oddly firm yet yielding beneath my boot and heard a strangely muffled grunt. Looking down I saw the back of a man's head and a young woman's face looking up at me. I had stepped on a courting couple in the grass! Both were too embarrassed to say much so I said, 'name the first one after me', and wandered on.

Vagrants in birding terms, those blown off course, usually on passage somewhere else, naturally enough occur during stormy weather or foggy conditions for example. So, be out and about after storms to see what might have blown your way.

It is worth mentioning here that species recording by the various nature conservation organisations has grown, with many people now involved in bird counts, butterfly recording, wildflower surveys and the like. This means that distribution maps of species are now much more accurate than ever they were but also, of course, they are often distribution maps showing the working areas of the keenest recorders. Despite gaps in the distribution maps of the commoner species they must be somewhere in the 10km squares, or whatever size tetrad is being used, but no one has actually sent in a record, thus the 'square' remains blank. Even as I write this in the year 2002 a recent Press Release stated that there are no records of house mice in Devon! A serious lapse on somebody's part.

There is also a marked tendency these days to record as 'extinct' species which may well not be, by the larger organisations involved, simply because they haven't and probably can't, cover all the possible terrain a rare or uncommon species might be breeding in.

Two cases in point in this past year or two, both involving bird species, are that "Cirl Buntings now only breed in South Devon", and "Red backed shrikes are extinct as a breeding species in the UK". Neither is correct at the time of writing this. I know of Cirl Buntings breeding in Somerset, for example, and of red backed shrikes nesting successfully in a railway cutting in Devon during 1999 and 2000. If data is to be correctly interpreted and information is to be accurate, "believed to be", might be a term better employed when referring to such matters. 'Extinct' is very final and the use of the term needs to be very carefully considered.

The above comments are not a criticism of the larger organisations. They cannot be everywhere. However they should take that fact on board and not assume extinctions quite so easily, nor that they know all there is to know.

16

Dread Times

Nature Conservation is not at all a light-hearted matter even though most of us involved in our different ways, try to be optimistic. Indeed if we were not so the probability that we are banging our heads against a brick wall would become more and more obvious.

Take oil pollution of our seas and oceans for example. I was involved in sea bird rescue in the 1970s when the Christos Bitos incident occurred and much oil was spilled, much of which came ashore in North Devon. Along with the oil came many hundreds of birds including razorbills and guillemots.

Our rescue group in North Devon consisted mainly of Jim Venner, from Nature Conservancy Council (NCC) Warden at Braunton Burrows, the late Jose Slee, a lovely lady who volunteered to help, and myself as the 'into the sea, catch and carry' people. The late Dr & Mrs Alan Stormont of Woolacombe, Devon helped carry oiled birds to the local rescue centre (unofficial) where Alan and Grace Jackson, of North Morte Farm helped feed, keep and clean them as we did so. We were more or less unofficial, though all Devon Bird Watching & Preservation Society members and deeply worried. Our link to bird preservation at that time was the RSPCA Unit at Hatch Beauchamp in Somerset who took the birds we had cleaned, fed and medicated from us. We few rescued about 2000 seabirds and only lost about 2%. Fantastic!

Jim Venner was told he shouldn't be out in the sea rescuing oiled birds. Jose Slee went out anyway, a superb person, and I went out up to my shoulders in the waves without telling either of them I could not swim. It did not matter. It was all about rescuing bird life and I took two weeks 'holiday' from work to do so. I would estimate the seven of us teamed up together 'saved' 1800-1900 birds.

We had wonderful back up. A local fresh fish shop gave us sprats and other fish free of charge for the birds. A local vet gave us the medicines to get into them and Alan and Grace gave them a cleaning facility and warm home on their farm situation prior to moving them to Somerset. I phoned Proctor and Gamble of Fairy Liquid fame and they gave us crates of the stuff free of charge to clean them with.

We worked all the daylight hours God gave us, ignoring our own home commitments for the sake of the oiled birds. Some of the sights we saw were quite terrible. I shall never forget them nor can one forgive the ridiculous situations that more or less permit these terrible oil pollution incidents to occur.

I was desperately anxious to find a protected area in North Devon at the time. It seemed to me we should cordon off some river site on the Taw from the possibility of oil coming in on the tide. The oil was around the coast and on the beaches. I phoned anxiously around but no one in authority, local government, conservation organisations or whatever would help. I phoned the then High Sheriff of Devon and explained the problem and the need. "Give me half an hour", he said. In about that time he phoned back to say a plastic boom was on its way by lorry, with motor cycle escort, to place it across Fremington Creek as I had requested. Sure enough, within an hour or so the boom had arrived and we installed it to at least keep oil on the tide from one tributary of the Taw River. The then Chief Executive of the Devon Wildlife Trust turned up to help and we got the whole thing into position. Wonderful, but to get it done I had to go 'to the top'.

Later, in my position as North Devon Rep for the RSPB , and Alan and Grace Jackson's help at Mortehoe, I instigated the first Oiled Bird Rescue System for the area, finding money enough for equipment including rescue nets, cleaning materials and infra red lamps to help keep the hapless creatures warm.

But why is Nature Conservation such an uphill struggle? At RAF Chivenor several years ago an incident involving aviation turbine fuel spillage caused another local wildlife disaster. At that time the spillage on the then RAF Fighter Training base leached into Braunton Marshes, the fumes alone causing those few of us involved in wildlife rescue, severe headaches and nausea. Again Helen Stormont and myself, together with the late Keith Mayhew, now North Devon's Dog Warden, spent many hours on site picking up sick mute swans and other creatures though to this day no real assessment of the mortality to wildlife has ever been made. Sadly Helen, Alan and Jose are now gone on ahead of the rest of us and very much missed, as is Keith.

These were major incidents, serious wildlife disasters and others around the UK over the years have shown this type of pollution is ever present. After the two incidents we found dead otters, hundreds of birds and other creatures strewn about at sites we had not been able to reach at the time. Today the RSPB has an annual Beached Bird Survey each February whereby many of us monitor a particular stretch of tidal river to see what is about. It is really a survey that provides a rough estimate of the ongoing problem. One hopes that in every county throughout the land there is an ever ready situation of people and equipment for these pollution problems which occur without warning and so swiftly take a toll on wildlife.

But now onto to other days. As the years passed I became owner of some land in North Devon which I set up as a private wildlife sanctuary. As it is some seven or eight miles from my home visits there meant packed lunches or a pasty in the local inn. Memories from those days have become "Tales From A Wayside Inn", all as it happened, more reminiscing...

PART TWO

Tales from a Wayside Inn

Introduction

The wayside inns and pubs all over the land provide a wealth of tales, some humorous, some sad, and all stops in between.

As well as providing drink, food, shelter and conversation, or even solitude if one seeks it and knows how to time it, the 'local' also provides a cross section of life rarely encountered with such richness and variety elsewhere under one roof.

Alcohol has nothing to do with it. Anyone in convivial mood be they ale or fruit juice drinkers may partake of the atmosphere of such places and simply enjoy.

The following tales are from memories of occasional visits to a favourite watering hole, which I had to pass, or not pass, en route twixt home and my wildlife sanctuary in the Westcountry. Once a farm the property became an inn many years ago and is set amidst rich countryside several miles from the nearest town and close to a number of scattered villages, hamlets and farms.

Modernised to some extent but in no way spoilt, mainly to provide excellent eating accommodation the inn has become popular with residents and visitors from all over the area as well as with the locals. A typical country pub one might say, happily retaining its rural atmosphere and character.

Some locals survive, the true, born in the area locals, along with 'locals' by choice and circumstance, 'furriners', as we say, who have moved with employment or retired to the area.

And along with the toing and froing of people come the tales and comments to ponder upon and be amused, amazed or charmed by, many of which I jotted down for just such a book as this.

Not fiction but absolutely true tales from a wayside inn then, put together from notes and memories that will have counter-parts all over the country, the essence of rural inn life. In compiling them many anecdotes were deliberately linked for story purposes but that is the only 'fictional' aspect of the book, other than that it all happened as I have set it out. The tales are related in a sort of seasonal order to provide some continu-ity which fits with my own coming and going in the area, thus several years of happy times will appear as but one year to the reader.

1

Springtime

It was one of those softly mild April evenings, primroses showing brightly in the hedgebanks along with left over celandines and wood anemones passed on by a cold and windy March. Spring was upon the countryside but it was raining. In fact it had been a wet winter, low lying fields swampy, the rivers and streams running high and ochre yellow with sediment, a mud on the boots time yet delightful with the knowledge and feel that spring had sprung.

Hurrying along the glistening darkly grey road hunched in my old Barbour and green wellies I saw the unmistakable, lean figure of Jack Piper up ahead of me stomping along as if he had all the time in the world, which I suppose he had.

Catching up with him I called, "Ow be'ee Knackin Jack?" in the well known locals peasant speech which we born locals are proud to keep going for the future whenever we meet up.

Jack grinned, his usually seriously set countenance lighting up with his great, jolly smile. "I'm priddy fiddy boy, and ow be you these days then?"

"I'm fine too", I replied. Are you going to hurry along with me then to get out of this rain?"

"Nope. Not much point. It's raining just as hard up front of us".

I slowed and walked with him. "Good to be getting back to lighter evenings don't you think?" I asked him.

"Now there I do agree with ee Tree", Jack replied, using my nickname given me many years past by an old friend. "Light evenings and nights are the best. Me and the missus loves to sit out in the garden on summer nights, nort better".

"Yes, you have a lovely garden Jack". He had shown me their garden many times as we carried mugs of hot, strong tea around with us admiring the well kept vegetable and flower beds of a real cottage garden tended with the loving care and instincts passed down from father to son, mother to daughter over the centuries.

Once I'd asked him if he used sprays to keep pests under control and received a blunt ticking off for even considering the possibility. Biological control, he had told me and in answer to my polite stare. "Pick 'em off and stamp on 'em lad".

Jack and his wife Sheila always planted properly according to moon phases, saying it was the reason everything in their garden thrived. Even the picking followed moon phases, just as was the way of it in the countryside generally many years ago. Sheila would say if it works it must be right. I heartily agree with them.

We entered the inn appropriately to the sound of Charlie Rich singing 'Behind Closed Doors' on the Juke Box.

"Must go and check me credentials", Jack muttered, heading off in the direction of the Gents as I glanced around to see a very elderly man in a very elderly black suit quietly staring at an empty glass on the bar before him.

"Hey Joe, haven't seen you for ages. What'll you have?" I asked him. Joe was an old timer of the area whom everyone liked.

"Six months. Over six months since you saw me in here last boy, and these days I'm all right thankee".

Joe accepted my offer of a drink, a Mackeson man like myself, a delightfully dark thirst quencher if ever there was one. Of Irish descent Joe McBride had been born, I knew, along the road at the old mill for he was proud of being its last resident and could tell many a tale of his younger days.

"Six months? You have a good memory Joe to remember when we last saw each other".

"Ad to be. I baint bin in here for six months. Been ill. They thought I was a goner". He quaffed his stout with relish.

"I'm sorry Joe, I had not heard you had been ill", I said.

"Nort much to 'ear about boy. I'm ninety. My father used to say death was nature's way of telling a body to slow down. I don't do much these days you know".

"Should hope not Joe", I replied as he settled back against the high backed, black stained wooden seat just inside the door, huge work-worn hands curled around his glass of dark nectar, a smile of contentment on his weather beaten face that was a lesson in living for anyone to learn from. I leaned back with him as Jack rejoined us with his pint of bitter.

Another voice piped up loud from the bar area.

"Cor, really ancient film on telly tonight. Elizabeth Taylor prefers horses to men". Bruce, a retired water bailiff with a lifelong knowledge of the countryside laughed as he swigged from his usual beer shandy.

Tweed jacket and moleskin trousers, always with shirt, tie and brogue shoes was Bruce's attire, a smart man with the glow of outdoor country life upon his face. Bruce was in for his weekly couple of hours at the inn. I asked him how he and his wife were even though he looked extremely well.

"Fair to middlin' Tree. Jenny's home mowing the lawn.

"Goodness. I thought that was your province Bruce", I said.

"Well yes, but I put up the bathroom scales by 7lbs for a joke like and she's been gardening like mad ever since".

I shook my head, smiling into the dark pool of Mackeson before me.

More Spring Memories.

"Where's everyone going?"

I aimed the question at Fred Harris who kept the little village shop, as we met in the road outside the inn. It was a delightful spring afternoon and I had earned a drink and ploughman's having planted a hundred native species trees on my steep hill slope that morning. A few people were walking along the road, chatting amiably but walking purposefully by the inn, obviously focussed, whilst cars passed with much tooting of horns and cheery waving.

"Football down at the field Tree. We are 'home' this Saturday."

"Didn't realise you got such a gate, Fred", I said as three more cars and a Land Rover passed us packed with people.

"Oh yes. We haven't won a match in 27 consecutive games. Drawn seven and lost twenty. It brings the crowds in".

I looked at him puzzled, opening the inn door to allow him access. We were the only customers. Fred saw my puzzlement and smiled.

"Well, Tree, nobody will miss a match now in case they miss the one we actually win".

We ordered food and drink. For me it was a lunch break after hard work at the Sanctuary, the delicious smell of hot pasties changing my mind away from a ploughman's, Fred doing the same.

The hot food arrived along with a Mackeson for me, and a bitter for Fred and we ate silently and appreciatively for a while.

"Hey, don't you sell these same pasties at the shop Fred? I asked as I recalled where else I had smelled the aroma of hot pasties.

"Aye, we do. The van delivers to both of us but they taste better up here with a bitter. Saturdays I always comes up for a quick one and drops in the bits and pieces they order from the shop. You must reciprocate custom in business Tree". Fred nodded at the ceiling, indicating the private quarters of the owners.

"Are these real Cornish pasties then, Fred?" I asked.

"Well, made to a Cornish pasty receipt". He used the old word for recipes as many country folk still do. "But they are made in Combe".

'Combe' is Ilfracombe to North Devonians, the still very popular seaside resort not many miles distant.

The pasties were certainly tasty and 'stayed' a person through the day quite adequately.

Just then the vicar walked in, accepting a glass of sherry graciously from the landlord.

"Church magazine time then vicar?" Fred called out.

"Yes Frederick, it is. I'll pop some into the shop later on my way to the match."

"Football fan then vicar?" I enquired.

"Not really Tree, but I keep up to date with local events where I can and when it isn't raining". He grinned. "Oh, I hear your daughter is pregnant Fred, congratulations. I married her in church you know", he added in an aside to me.

"Yes, she's four months on now vicar. It weren't planned but they are happy about it".

"More of a side effect then Fred", I said. Fred guffawed and the vicar cast me a reproving glance.

"Aye, you're right there Tree. Good one that, vicar?"

"Er, yes. Shan't use it myself though Frederick". He shook his head at me but there was a twinkle in his eyes.

"Well must be on my way. Thank you for the sherry Brian, must get to the match and all that, we might win this week".

Brian the landlord chuckled. "Best tell them to play in half time then vicar, while the other side are sucking lemons"

We all chuckled as the reverend gentleman went on his jovial way, as Charles Squire came into the bar. Captain of the inn's darts team Charles worked for a largish firm in the nearby town and had moved to the village some four years previously when his mother had died leaving him the family home. Charles and his wife had slotted quickly into village life, the locals remembering his boyhood days there and all loving his parents from years before.

Charles hated being called Charlie, a well known fact which had been used to good effect by visiting teams hoping to get him off guard for he was a very good darts and pool player, known for 'throwing good arrows' and earning his place in the team.

"Fancy a game Tree?"

Startled from my contemplation of the remaining liquid in my glass, and nudged encouragingly by Fred I rose reluctantly from my comfortable seat feeling my muscles aching from the earlier tree planting. I am no darts player, preferring to play a quiet game of pool though I am no pool player either.

"Alright then Charles"? I heard myself saying as Brian handed me a set of old fashioned feathered flighted darts from behind the bar. I walked to assume the position and threw three darts casually as a warm-up swiftly at the board. All three went into the 20 position with one at double top. I stared fascinated sure I would have hit random areas of the board. Fred said "lumme" out loud and Brian leaned on the bar to watch.

Charles stared at me. "Been practising then Tree?" I said I had not as he walked over to the scoreboard, marked up 301 and deducted my 80. I had thought it was a sort of warm-up throw but decided to let it go with the Gods while I still had a chance.

Charles unsheathed his personal darts and took aim.

"No. No Charlie, I don't practice at all" I said.

Charles' first dart hit the 5 beside the 20. He glared at me but I was gazing about. The next dart hit the treble 20 and he grinned widely.

"Been practising then Charlie? I asked.

"Charles, 'tis Charles", he grated, and hit the 5 again. Deducting his 70 he stood aside for me.

"Loser buys the drinks Tree", Charles said as I threw.

I watched the dart drop away from its intended trajectory and inwardly groaned. It fell into treble 19!

The shock rendered Charles quiet. I grinned and took careful aim. Another 20 and deliberate this time. 77 scored. I didn't care about the next and let fly. In total disbelief we watched it thud into the 25 ring.

"102 Charles old chap", I said as casually as I could muster. Fred and Brian stared as if I was something from outer space.

"Jammie tonight Tree, Aren't you", Charles muttered as he took aim.

"Actually Charles I'm thinking of the News of the World".

Charles dart dropped into the 3 as if shocked away from hitting the 20 directly above.

"The News of the World!" Charles exploded. But that's the big time in darts". His next dart hit the 1 spot.

"That's 4," I called.

"I can count. But what is this about the 'News of the World'?" Charles took several gulps of his Poachers Bitter.

"The newspaper, not their darts tournament, good Lord I'm no darts player Charles".

Three of Charles' team mates came into the bar. It must be practice time I thought, probably a match that night.

Bert Champion, one of the team came over. "Tree's got you on the run Charlie, I mean Charles."

Charles third dart headed for the 20 and hit the wire, ricocheting onto the bar. Fred and the others did a bit of exaggerated hiding from the danger area. Fred shouted at Charles to stop gaming about whilst Bert marked up the 4 score, shaking with suppressed mirth. I stared hard at the board, 119 left to my opponents 227. I could not believe it. I threw again at the 20 spot, the dart flying to the right but into the treble 18. I looked skywards then threw the next dart right into the 5, to the left. Logic said aim for the 1. I did and logic won for I hit the 20. Bert marked up 40 for me to get. The bar went as quiet as the grave. Charles took a drink and threw. He hit 20, treble 20 then the Bull. Bert called 130. They were beautiful darts. Charles was rightly pleased as we grinned at each other.

"Go for it you hustler", he said.

My first dart hit the board outside and above the 20 area, hanging loose. I aimed at the feathers and threw, my dart hitting the 20 double spot and hanging there sagging like the first.

What's your poison Tree?" Charles came over grinning as both my darts fell to the floor as if exhausted.

"The usual Mackeson please, and thanks".

I sat down glad it was over, knowing when Lady Luck had smiled.

2

The Professor

Whether he was or had been a professor no one really knew. He'd come quietly to live in the village in a large, secluded cottage screened by trees. He was from Sussex someone said. 'The Professor' certainly had the right image. Studious looking, those gold rimmed pince nez, tweed suited and a mildly pleasant absent minded sort of manner that one associated with that fine actor Alistair Simms somehow.

Ted a local builder said he'd had men in the house for four weeks with lots of timber and stuff going in but the workmen had come from the town and had taken their secrets with them.

I first met him along the road. I'd been working on a butterfly survey in the valley and was timing myself nicely for a ploughman's lunch to remove the hollowness of a morning without breakfast and stop my belly and my backbone bumping, as they say.

He was watching two male orange tip butterflies flitting along the hedge, crouched and intent on his observations.

"Lovely aren't they" I remarked as I drew level.

Ah yes, a delight and so common around here".

"Lots of Jack-by-the-hedge and Ladies Smock around here", I told him referring to the foodplants of the species.

"Ah, you know your butterflies then, good. I am growing sweet rocket and honesty in the garden also, to attract them but nothing like the natural foodplant really". His eyes gleamed with enthusiasm.

"I'm on my way to the inn for a ploughman's, why not join me?" I suggested.

He hesitated briefly, then, "Yes, I don't usually but a change is as good as a rest and all that. Let me get a jacket".

Twenty minutes later we were seated on sun-warmed benches in the garden area of the inn with excellent cheddar ploughmans and a Mackeson before each of us. We chatted butterflies and birdlife, finding a mutual interest in the wildlife and our concern for the future of the countryside.

He told me he had moved to the Westcountry away from the English dustbowl areas of the eastern counties, from the pollution and the intensity of the arable farming. A 'retire and retreat' he called it, remarking on how fortunate we were in the Westcountry.

We chatted, setting the world to rights as people do when passionate about anything.

"We will pay dearly my friend", he said, "if we do not see the way we are going and put it to rights very quickly".

A cock crowed in the distance, a lovely country sound as much in decline as otters and barn owls. I said as much.

"Yes, I love the sound and much respected it was in the countryside as herald of the dawn when countryfolk used to be up with the sun. Do you know, in Abysinnia they were kept in churches in order to wake the villagers?"

I told him I did not know that but that the birds were always connected with the Gods and sacred to Appollo the Sun God. Tis said the cock's crowing summoned the God from sleep to pursue his daily task of driving the sun across the heavens in his chariot.

"Yes, yes, wonderful, and it was Athene who had the emblem of a cock on her helmet, such a magnificent bird, the cockerel I mean not Athene". He laughed aloud, his quiet manner hiding a lovely sense of humour.

I reminded him also that the identification of the cock with the sun accounted for the old country belief that hen's eggs would be addled if there was thunder about during incubation.

We chatted a while longer but time was ever the enemy and we glanced at our watches simultaneously.

"I must away", he said, "I have straggled from my daily activities but it was well worth it. We must do this again. Time is a martinet is it not". He smiled as we went our separate ways happily enjoying the peace of the place and the butterflies along the way.

3

'Chippy' Kerswell

C hippy' Kerswell was the local carpenter, a Jack-of-all-trades really but excellent at his work which rather tossed out the old adage about 'master of none'. He had served as undertaker in the area long enough to fill the churchyard he reckoned. 'Chippy' was a dour looking fellow with the dry wit that often comes with such looks and was liked immensely in the area both for his character and his workmanship for he could do most anything with timber, a true craftsman of his day.

He had a way of looking a person up and down then directly in the eyes as if taking stock before getting to the nitty gritty. Quite likely he was taking a person's measure at the same time.

'Chippy' was always spotlessly turned out in pristine navy blue overalls and a navy suit jacket, his one touch of sartorial elegance being a 'loud' checked trilby hat he wore to the back of his head to show off a mop of silver-grey hair. A tall man he was slightly stooped and gaunt, deeply tanned and with twinkling blue eyes that had never needed spectacles. He kept bees in five white hives in his large garden orchard, swearing by the health giving properties of the honey they gave. He would not sell it but if you passed muster with him 'Chippy' would slip a jar into your hand once or twice in a year and wonderful stuff it was.

'Chippy' had an older brother living on the Quantocks who wrote every month.

"Regular as clockwork be Tom, even when there's nothing to say and he always signs his letter 'eventually yours' the cheeky beggar", he laughed.

A half pint of light ale arrived on the bar top, the landlady knowing his usual tipple. He stared at her in his dry old manner.

"Mine's a bitter shandy tonight m'dearie", he said.

June raised her eyebrows and swiftly exchanged the drinks.

'Chippy' smiled at me. "You mustn't let em take ee for granted must ee lad", he said.

June grinned at me over his shoulder. The acoustics behind the bars of England are pretty good. There isn't much missed in those strategic places. She bustled about preparing for the usual early movement of customers.

"Had your hair done then me dearie?" Chippy suddenly said to her.

I stared. Sure enough June was sporting an immaculate hairdo, shorter than usual, though she was always a very smart woman.

"Oh, can you tell?" She smiled happily.

"Aye, said 'Chippy', always leaves you ladies with red faces do them hair dryer things. My missus be the same."

He deftly dodged the swinging glass-cloth June was using, as the landlord arrived laughing at the comment and not so lucky as to avoid the follow through.

A group of eight youngsters arrived, freshly modern in shirts, blouses and blue denim jeans, the uniform of the young. Laughing and jostling they spread about the bar like newly emerged dragonflies in an established old pond, ordering their drinks loudly as they set the pool balls rattling and the juke box playing some throbbing music.

'Chippy' and I called out our goodbyes to stroll the peaceful evening road outside.

"Funny old world", he mused. "Cant buy sugar in pounds anymore but we still have ale in pints."

"It's nice to hang on to some of the old things in life", I replied.

"You sound like the vicar at a WI meeting". He laughed. "Talking of that did I ever tell ee about the last night George was landlord of the pub before Brian took it on?"

I said I hadn't heard of the night.

"Well we had a little do after hours and we gives him and his missus a fine dinner service. There was a fair old load of empties as you'll imagine so I said I'd help clear up when the others had gone home. We did a lot of clearing when suddenly George said to pop the boxes of empties into the car, which us did and ee said to hop in. Anyways us went up the road to the vicar's place and George stopped very quietly outside. Twas pitch dark and George said we'll fill the dustbin and leave the rest all about it, it's collection day tomorrow. Cor, 'twas talk of the village for nigh on a week but the vicar's a rare old sport. Well, you've got to have a sense of humour when you have to wear your shirt wrong way round aven't ee lad".

A lovely man, 'Chippy' rest his soul.

4

A Reverend Gentleman

I first met the vicar to speak to at about the same spot in the road where the professor and I had met up some time before. I was standing facing into the hedgerow watching an Elephant Hawkmoth on rosebay willowherb. It was a superb summers day and I heard this rather gentle cough to draw my attention.

"God, you startled me", I exclaimed recognising his collar as I spoke, realising at the same time that I might have chosen a safer comment.

"I'm merely the vicar actually". The smile was benign, the round, pleasant smooth face shining, the eyes large and dark brown.

"I see you are observing Mother Nature's miracles then", he continued, "And they are hereabouts in abundance".

"Well, yes, that's part of what I do", I answered as we introduced ourselves. I discovered he read my wildlife articles in a local paper.

We talked of a former clergyman of the area who had written quite a lot about the local wildlife, a Reverend Ball, and about the changes since then.

It is good to see someone stop and take notice of their surroundings", he said. "So many miss their share of happiness, not because they do not find it but because they do not stop to enjoy it once found".

"Too true", I agreed. "Some do tend to pass the best of life by, by being blinkered and in a rush through life".

"Quite so". His eyes shone eagerly. "I must write a sermon around it. By the way I don't see you in church do I". It was a statement rather than a question.

"No you don't", I confirmed. "I must say I find my Maker more in the countryside amongst the trees and lanes and am happy with that. And do you find your homily each week in the things you see everyday then?" I asked him.

"Well serendipity plays a large part. Even you artists find it so do you not?"

"Happy accidents. Of course, I have reaped the benefits of those with my watercolour work. Do you have many? Say in your job at the font?"

He stared at me aghast.

What had I said? I found myself struggling for words.

"I mean, say, at a Christening", I continued

He continued to stare. I began to feel uneasy. "Do you never get the Christian names mixed up at all?" I persisted.

"Ah, I see". He laughed nervously, seeming relieved at my genuine explanation. It now dawned on me what I had said and how he had taken it but I restrained any laughter on my part.

The vicar looked skywards in contemplation. "Yes. Well let me see. The worst I've done is to get names in the wrong order but it is rare, I am not a recidivist".

"I'm glad to hear it", I said heartily, mentally storing the word to memory for a quick check of the dictionary later. "Do you have a large flock?" I continued.

He smiled and sighed deeply. "The sheep farmers hereabouts do better than I but then, they purchase theirs".

"Not always. There's lambing of course", I reminded him.

"Yes there is". He looked at me closely as if to see if I was being flippant, which I wasn't. "There were traffic jams on the road here on Easter Sunday, vehicles milling about all over the place trying to find the church. It was such a beautiful spring day. The human memory doesn't last from one year to the next it seems". He smiled a little ruefully. "Do you know, I had a notice put in the church porch which said YOU MUST PAY FOR YOUR SINS' and someone wrote beneath it, 'IF YOU HAVE ALREADY PAID PLEASE DISREGARD THIS NOTICE'.

"Dearie me", was all I could muster in reply.

"Where are you going now by the way? He asked.

"To the inn. I have a pasty or a ploughman's when I'm working here at the Sanctuary". I told him.

"Then I'll walk with you, the Parish Magazine you see". He held up a wodge of little books. "Tell me what else you do on this wildlife theme".

We chatted of my paintings and writing as we walked. He told me of his own attempts and that the good Lord had not endowed him with the gift of painting. He told me how he had once done several little watercolour scenes and put them around the vicarage lounge. One afternoon a parishioner who was also a good artist had called and he noticed she kept casting furtive glances at the paintings. Finally she asked him who did them.

He grinned at me. "I told her they were all my own work and breathing a sigh of relief she said she was really glad I had not paid any money for them".

He chuckled and as we chatted on he recalled the night of the many bottles in and around his dustbin.

"Funny thing was", he said, "that very night my wife was elected WI President and it was at breakfast she pondered on whether it might take up too much of her time. Well dear, I told her, the first thing you have to learn is to delegate responsibility".

"Oh I knew you would be sweet about it dear, she said to me. You empty the rubbish bin and wash up then while I dash off to the coffee morning in the village. And that's when I discovered the bottles. I was at the bin when the refuse collection vehicle arrived and believe you me there were some sniggles and dropped jaws about. Oh and I remember, talking of sniggles, I think the funniest moment at a wedding was when after I had said wilt thou take this woman for thy lawfully wedded wife, the groom said, I wilt. Mind you, there was also the little girl being shown around the church by her parents. My wife went to assist, finding they were on holiday in the area and showed them the beautiful carved screen saying it was a 16th century rood screen.

The little girl shouted to her mummy not to look if it was a rood screen. It took a little while to explain to her that rood refers to the crucifix atop the actual screen but we got there in the end".

We wandered into the inn, which was pleasantly cool and shaded, sunlight beams entering the low windows casting bright rectangles across the deep red-carpeted floor. A young man glanced up and recognised the vicar's attire. He looked hard at his girlfriend, then at the barmaid.

"Er, two orange juices please", he said.

I was grinning. The girlfriend had her back to us and in strident tones she said, "ere, I don't want no orange juice, not unless there's a large gin in it".

"Orange juice is better this time of day", growled the young man.

June the barmaid grinned. "Two orange juices it is then".

"Cor luv a duck, ave you run out of cash then Jimmie? I've got some money luv".

The young man went scarlet then burst out laughing. He turned to the vicar. "You see reverend, the old dog collar works wonders, but orange juices are fine".

The girl turned and almost curtsied. "Coo, you might ave said Jimmie. I wouldn't down yer like that".

"You just down the drink and let's get in a game of pool".

They wandered off to the pool room, scene of many a pub battle, the rumble of dropping balls accompanied by "I Want To Be Free" blaring from the juke box.

"Whoever is that singing?" the vicar asked me as we raised our glasses of Mackeson in cheerful salutation.

"That's the Queen", I replied blandly, airing my scant knowledge of modern pop stars.

"Is it indeed, and I suppose Prince Philip does the encores". He looked at me a little perplexed at what he thought was my odd sense of humour.

I left it where it was.

Fred & Co.

Fred Norman was henpecked 'twas said. Everyone in the village knew it was so. Even Fred himself was heard to say if he wanted to know what his wife wanted doing next all he had to do was sit down.

Jessie Norman, Fred's wife had a temper. "Best to let her be". Fred would say, but she also had a heart of gold to go with it especially if anyone was in trouble.

Fred 'escaped' to the inn once a week whilst Jessie went playing whist, or to the WI, or to see her mother who was alive still at 97.

"Deaf as a post her mother is", Fred said many a time. "So I don't go along to hear shouting, I can stay home and do that". He grinned a sly sort of grin for everyone knew Jessie was a good sort unless something or someone crossed her, and one of the best cooks for miles around.

Part of Jessie's trouble was that she was house proud. If Fred was gardening, and woe betide any weeds that invaded their garden, there were always newspapers in the hall even though he kept his gardening boots in the shed. This stemmed from the one and only time Fred didn't. He'd cut himself badly with secateurs and had rushed in for First-Aid with his boots on.

"And with blood dripping as well", Jessie was quick to remind everyone.

This evening, a hot and sultry night during summer lambing time, the inn was quiet and I was drinking orange juice for the sheer refreshment and taste of it.

"Drinking strong stuff aint you boy?" Fred grinned at me. "Be ee sure you can handle it then?"

A huge man leaned on the bar with a menu in his hand and laughed as he heard Fred's remark to me.

"Two salads and two large scotches landlord", he boomed. He looked at my fruit juice. "The three Ss man, salad, scotch and sex, that's the secret of a happy and healthy life".

I looked across the bar to the large, attractive woman he was with. She shrugged across at me and smiled.

"Well, you only ordered two of the three as I recall", I said.

"And if rabbits drank whisky then think how long they'd live according to your theory".

"Mmm. True enough that", muttered the large man, his booming tones muted.

Fred was laughing in his asthmatic way, not that he suffered from the malady, just that he laughed like the cartoon character Mutley, almost stifled and with his body shaking in time.

"Big woman that", Fred said. "Reminds me of Jessie's sister.

Jessie's sister was a former matron of the Hattie Jaques type who sailed into the village for a two weeks stay every summer.

"Sometime back when car seat belts wasn't compulsive", Fred said. He had a beautiful way with slight word errors that never lost the context of what he was saying. Jessie's Marion was down here on holiday when her car broke down and she borrowed ours to go shopping in town. Marion was a stickler for wearing seat belts and our little Morris 1000 didn't have any at the time. Anyways, she drove into town, parked against the kerb, did her usual routine of undoing the belt, got out on the pavement and her skirt fell down. Fred went off into one of his paroxysms of almost silent mirth.

"She's quite a wag though", he continued. "We all went into town one day to B......s," he named a large store which sold quality clothing, perfumes and all kinds of accessories for women. "Well Marion tried on two or three coats and they were all too tight, so she asks the assistant if they'd got anything larger in the same size. The assistant went and had a look too. That reminds me. Marion will be down in a week for her annual holiday. That'll mean some late nights as she loves her adult films. You know the ones, where adults act like kids most of the time".

"There's something in what you say Fred". I agreed. "And where rich people are always miserable with their lot."

"That's it Tree. Like that daft oil family soap that's so popular. Chap in the village asked me what I thought was going to happen to one of the characters. I told'n I know what would happen to him if I wrote the script."

Fred ordered another round, grinning as I remained on fruit juice.

"What do ee call a hangover from fruit juice then Tree? " he laughed.

"A drupe, I suppose", I replied, which I thought was pretty good on the spur of the moment.

"There was some excitement down in the village last week, quite a crowd around the shop, some chap had dropped daid in the road. Mind you it wasn't as bad as us thought, 'twas only a visitor".

I looked at Fred. He was staring into his glass. I smiled inwardly for his comment was a straightforward one. It was the way of it. Those you don't know cant mean as much as those you do. I guess it's why we can watch the TV news without much flinching.

Horace Jones wandered into the bar in his usual bustling way.

Horace was of Welsh extraction, the Welsh accent becoming quite pronounced still, when Horace was emotional. He was a jolly sort, short and stocky, always neat and tidy, a blazer and badge on breast pocket man who had recently retired from the railways. In celebration he had brought his alarm clock and a sledgehammer to the inn for his retirement party, placed the clock on the Beer Garden tarmac and dealt it a mighty blow in public.

"There lads", he said, "That's a blow for freedom now and for not having to get up at unearthly hours in the future".

There was an uneasy silence and the little crowd of friends who had gathered, glasses in hand to witness the scene glanced sheepishly at each other as the landlord stepped forward. What was to come, I wondered, as I hovered at the back of the gathering. I was not a local in the proper sense for I did not reside in the village and this was village business.

"Horace. It is your retirement today and as one of our valued customers and long member of the darts team we had a little whip round. This is from all of us to mark your retirement and we wish you a long and peaceful one."

Brian the landlord handed Horace a neatly tied parcel, a beaming smile on his face, as everyone applauded heartily.

"Well, well, well, what a lovely surprise everybody. I'll open it now then shall I?" Horace was smiling happily as he took the parcel and began opening it.

I seemed to feel the silence as Horace revealed a rectangular box and smiling with anticipation opened it and pulled out, to his utter amazement, an alarm clock.

Horace stared at the clock, then at each face in the crowd in turn. He stared at the sledgehammer leaning against the wall and then he burst out laughing.

"Drinks are on me everyone", he shouted and we all trooped back into the inn's cosy interior.

Amidst noisy jollification Brian asked Horace if he'd retired at 60 or 65.

"65 last August Brian, but fit as a flea, though I did have some trouble with the doctor because of pains in my chest a while ago.

The doc' ran the old stethoscope over me, tapped my chest and back a bit like they do, then he said he couldn't find any cause for the pains and it must be due to drink. I said to him, well I'll come back when you're sober then. He didn't take too kindly to that mind you."

Joan Jones, his wife came over. For years she had borne the brunt of her unfortunate name but in good heart. She was a pleasant, pretty woman who followed the old traditions of hats to be worn on Sundays and all that.

"Hello Tree, how are you then?" She asked in her quiet voice.

"Fine Joan, as ever. Haven't seen you in here for a while".

She smiled and winked. "No Tree, last time me and Horace went out together the kitchen stove had caught fire". She chuckled.

"Rubbish, we used to go out a lot dear", Horace said.

"Yes, during the war when you were on leave love. Actually Tree, I love the garden and a bit of telly and we go out weekends".

"An Army man through the war then Horace?" I asked him.

"Yes, all through. Came off a farm, volunteered. Six years. A doddle really. I remember the lads all groaning at having to get up at 6.30am in training and of course it was an extra hour in bed for me cos I used to be up to milk the cows in civvy street by 5.30 am every day."

"What's a three letter word for proverb?" Brian called out. He was doing the newspaper crossword, a dangerous thing to do as his wife always liked to do it. "Begins with S" he added.

"Saw", I said.

"Saw? That's for cutting wood, or past tense for see", Horace said.

A conversation about the oddities of the English language began in earnest.

They say 'tis the hardest language of all to learn." Said Joan.

"Probably is", Horace said. "Harder than Welsh. I remember at school my teacher saying, sit there for the present Horace Jones, and I sat in that chair for the whole term without seeing the present I was waiting for".

"Silly old fool." Joan laughed. "Well you got one today so there".

5

Henry & I

enry and I had decided to meet up for a natter to bring ourselves up to date with one another as was our wont whenever possible. I found him leaning on the farm gate across the road from the inn's front door, gazing across the valley. He was his usual natty self in a grey tweed suit and brogue shoes, check shirt, and wool tie, his steel grey hair combed and full, but there was a slump to his shoulders as he leaned.

"How is it then Henry?" I called and at the sound of my voice he straightened up in military fashion. Not a man to show he was feeling down was Henry.

He stared into my eyes with his own brightly blue, startlingly clear eyes. "I'm alright Tree my friend. Bit iffy on the home front. Wife's banging rather hard on the typewriter, which means the writing isn't coming along too well. When I asked what she was writing she said her bloody resignation from our marriage. Perhaps I should accept it."

There was not a lot I could say to that.

"Mmm. Why don't we both take her a bottle of wine and cheer her up". I suggested.

"Not a chance". He shook his head. Three women from the play-acting group there now. When one is outnumbered best tactics are to do a flanker, let things ease."

We wandered into the inn. Only three people in and strains of Mick Jagger stating he, 'cant get no satisfaction' from the Juke Box.

"Mackeson for Tree and a Bitter for me landlord please", Henry said.

"Good to see you Henry", Brian said as he poured the drinks while we leaned on the polished bar.

'Chippie' the local carpenter could be seen puttying one of the bar windows from outside in the Beer Garden. He grinned cheerily and waved his putty knife.

"Broken window then landlord", Henry asked.

"No, that's the mended one. Chippie took the broken one out". Brian was his usual cheery self. "Boy from the village put a stone through it. Cheeky whelp. I asked him how he came to hit the window and he said his catapult went off while he was cleaning it."

Henry chuckled. "A boy of some imagination and wit. No animus I'm sure". Henry had as usual produced a word to fit the occasion.

"Animus? As animosity Henry?" Brian asked him.

"Yes. Hostile intent. Probably testing its powers as did we all as boys I suppose."

Voices across the bar rose in heated conversation. Six people had drifted in, sat around an old oak table and were in animated conversation on Europe and the Third World.

"Strange isn't it," Henry said, "Only one person in a million really understands the international situation and they all come in here on the same night".

'Chippie' came in, his glazing job finished.

"What'll you have chippie?" I called.

"Just an orange juice thanks, I'm driving the pick-up. Lots of windows to repair this week".

Henry guffawed. "Ah, your hired hand going round with a catapult eh?"

"No. Not my favourite job. Hard old putty. Hey Tree, you haven't talked to our WI have you? They'd love a wildlife talk."

"No I haven't chippie. But you aren't a member are you?"

"My wife's secretary. Good, Then I'll tell her you've agreed then shall I". It was a statement.

"Alright, an hour or so on wildlife, but in the autumn. Give me time to think about it".

"Done. She'll be pleased as Punch". He drank up, waved and went on to his next port of call.

Henry picked up three feathered darts from the block on the bar-top. "Fancy a game?" he said, throwing two 20s and a double 20 in rapid succession.

"Not tonight," I grinned. "Rather just watch the sunset".

Henry chuckled. "Just as well. I'm off form. Come on then Tree, let's take a bottle of red wine home to my wife and cheer her up".

6

Amos

It was one of those splendid spring evenings with swallows, swifts and house martins screaming with joy as they hurtled after high flying insects over farmland where lambs gambolled about lush grass growth as their mother ewes grazed contentedly nearby. A half a dozen of us were in the Beer Garden drinking tall orange squashes after I'd led a pleasant field trip to see what birdlife was about in the area. It had been a perfect afternoon and warm from walking we found the drinks more than welcome.

Amos from the village store came out from the shady interior of the inn and I beckoned him over to sit with us. Amos was the typical village store keeper, white shirt and waistcoat, a National Trust tie of green with oak acorns and black suit trousers. He wore his shirt sleeves rolled back to show strong arms, tanned with years of country living.

"Good to get out", he smiled. He looked tired but pleased to join us and sipped the beer shandy he had brought with him into the sunshine. I asked how his family was.

"Missus and daughter both well thanks. Like two puddings with that sickly sauce from the TV pouring all over them mind you. They have all their adventures in that little box." He shook his head.

Amos has a lovely wife and daughter, she about 30 and still at home. They all worked hard at the business but it was well known he was a TV widower at night.

"What will it be tonight then Amos?" I asked him gently.

"Coronation Street. They wont miss it. They believe it. They talk about the characters and worry about them. Emotionally involved they gets. The other day I came home in the middle of a conversation in the shop. Four of 'em talking about somebody being ill, same name as one of the villager's. That person came into the shop next day and I made a fool of myself commiserating with them over their illness which they never had of course". Still, I get to read a lot, which I enjoy. The travelling library comes round, really good that, a minor social event as several villagers enjoy a good read".

Brian was serving the field trippers next to us. "Wasn't there some fuss up at the van last week Amos?" he asked. News travels in small village areas, especially at the inn.

"That's right. Talk of changing the days. About a dozen of us regulars turned up. Bit awkward, half agreeing with the proposed change and the others wanting the day to remain as it was. Quite niggly it became".

"Aschism", I said.

"Bless you", Amos said grinning broadly, "You should take something for that ".

Brian stifled his merriment. I shut up.

My field trippers were on their feet saying their thank yous and goodbyes, suitably refreshed. I saw them off and resumed my place beside Amos.

He continued. "As it was they decided to keep the day as it has been for ages so I was well pleased".

I asked him what type of books he enjoyed. He told me detective tales, Conan Doyle's Sherlock Holmes he loved, and for a change, Ellery Queen, Hammett, and Peter Cheyney. He said he loved to use Holmesian methods on people who come in to his shop or the inn if he didn't know them too well.

"Oh, really? That would be something to do now Amos." Brian said. He was sitting at the next table there being no customers inside.

"You're on", Amos agreed, and as if on cue Henry arrived limping very slightly and with a stick. He came across smiling as I went to get him a drink and replenish mine. On my return with Brian I nodded to Amos to begin his Holmesian methods of deduction.

"Let me see." He eyed my old friend up and down carefully. "I'd say you have fallen, your shoe is scuffed across the toe cap and you always have them shiny, so it was recent. The walking stick isn't yours, belongs to a shorter man who has a dog. You don't usually walk about with a book so I would say you've borrowed it and as it isn't library van day you have either just borrowed it or are taking it back to the owner". Amos sat back smiling.

Henry looked at us and nodded. "Spot on thus far Amos". He smiled. "So what else can you tell from the book and stick?"

Amos took up the stick, warming now to his task. "The dog bit was easy. Teeth marks see, and a small dog, terrier or spaniel type from the marks. The book is a bit of a guess but I'd say it is the stick owners book because it is about sheepdogs and terriers." Again he leaned back.

"Right again Amos. Jack Russell actually, the dog."

Henry was smiling as he spoke, obviously enjoying the moment.

"In fact everything you say is accurate Amos old chap".

Brian and I were eying Amos incredulously.

Amos looked at us and chuckled. " It was easy really. You see, Henry came into our shop earlier and tripped over the step. He was a bit shaken so the missus makes him a cuppa and he spent an hour in the parlour easing his ankle. Of course the stick and book he borrowed from me, the Jack Russell is our dog Jake. "

"Then I drove here as Henry felt like walking on such a nice day".

Brian's bar-cloth hit him across the ear.

Amos laughed. "But I do love Sherlock Holmes, Really"

"Give him a refill on me please Brian, and for all of us. I reckon we deserve it," I had to admit.

7

Bert, Martha & All...

I had spent the morning clearing a fallen tree from across my woodland path. Why do trees fall the wrong way? All the same I enjoyed the physical work, levering the trunk with a crow bar inch by inch until it was safely off the path then banging in a few stout stakes to keep it from slipping. The path itself I had dug years before along the side of the steep slope of the woods. It had taken me six hot, hard days but I could now walk quietly and watch the wildlife without slipping down over the slope and frightening the animals. I could also see most of my nestboxes from the same path and could therefore monitor them without undue disturbance. Indeed, the wild animals used the path a lot, especially the deer and the vixen who lived in an earth in the woods and had her cubs there. Now it was just a matter of maintaining it, which was generally an easy task.

There was always so much to see that I was loathe to leave the Sanctuary for it is also such a peaceful place but I had other things to do and sometimes food and drink beckoned, particularly after heavy toil.

The thought of a Mackeson was too good to resist and thus it was that noontime saw me catching up with Bert from the next village and we entered the inn together.

"Fashion! Just look at that".

I glanced to where Bert nodded with a somewhat less than approving glance.

A young couple sat in a corner looking a little ill at ease, that sort of first date or first time in a pub look, I thought. The girl was very pretty but her hair was frizzed out of any semblance of naturalness, as if she'd caught hold of a 1000 volt cable.

"All the rage, very trendy Bert", I grinned.

He nodded. "Fashion. It's what people want today, didn't like yesterday and won't touch tomorrow. It aint real. If some film star does summat different tomorrow the sheeps of fashion will follow."

"Sheep, not sheeps", I said.

Bert stared at me. "No I mean sheeps, not just one sheep, lots of them. Sheeps."

"I see," I replied, "and how's your good lady Bert?"

Bert thrust his hands deep into his baggy cord trousers held with a wide leather belt holding a well fed belly in place. A dreamy look came over the round shaven face then he patted the tartan check shirt he was wearing and smiled.

"Er be fine lad. Baking today, Smelled the fresh braid and cakes as I came home along the road earlier. Nort better".

I had to agree. Fresh baked country bread. Lovely.

We sipped our drinks to 60s songs on the Juke Box. "Lazin On A Sunny Afternoon' sang The Kinks. I recalled the group well and pleasantly harmonious they were. They had conquered the pop world by wearing Hunting Pink on stage. The world suddenly noticed them. I mused on what the hunting landowners around here would have thought had the Kinks turned up for a Meet on horseback.

"Penny for them Tree"...the words startled me from my daydreaming.

Joy and Peter who lived in a converted farm building on the outskirts of the parish were smiling at my vacant expression.

"Where were you?" Joy asked

"Just away with the music folks. How are you and what's your poison?"

"Thanks. Half a lager each would do nicely," smiled Peter, a rather debonair character, ex RAF who sported fine shirts and a cravat and always looked right in them. Joy lived up to her name, a willowy blonde who always caught the eye in tight blouses and slacks, a lovely couple who had moved with the RAF to a nearby camp from which Peter had since retired to country life.

With mine and Bert's glasses refilled the four of us sat in a window seat enjoying the view outside across a tiny garden.

Joy said, "We had a laugh today. Our daughter Janie rang from university and had us really worried".

"I thought you said 'laugh'?" I queried.

"Well yes, she proudly announced she's top of her class, at the new sex education course!"

There was little to say to that. The 'new' young couple were giggling, having overheard. I raised my glass to them, receiving shy nods in return.

Joy asked after Bert's wife. He told her about the baking session, then said.

"We went up to Exeter last Saturday. Coach trip from town. A real treat. Looked around the cathedral, saw a Bishop doing his bit. First time I've seen a real crook".

Joy giggled and Peter looked shocked.

"Aye", Bert continued. "I've seen a few shepherd's crooks in my day but never a Bishop's".

Bert carried on unaware of our smiles. "Glad to get home though. Couldn't live in a city. Went to this art exhibition just as some chap was judging children's paintings. Some lovely stuff they'd done. He picked this picture of flowers by a little girl as the winner. She came up for her prize and he went on about colour sense and then he said the main reason for choosing hers was its freedom and spontaneity, he loved spontaneous work. Then he asks the little girl how long she had taken to complete it.

She told him for all the world to hear that she's done it on her fifth try. Four times she'd copied it then she gave up and traced it. Real spontaneous that was, but kids are funny. Last week a cub scout called for Bob-a-Job week. Missus said come in and peel these potatoes and she would make him a cup of tea. Anyway when he'd finished I paid him a few shillings and he asked if we would put 'shifting dustbins' on his sheet and not peeling potatoes. I asked him why and he says cos his mother would read the card and she didn't need to know he could peel potatoes.

Peter and Joy wandered off to play their everlasting darts

tournament just as the door swung open and in walked Ivy and Martha, two buxom sisters who had a way of suddenly being there, all smiles, fresh air and lavender scents.

"Must be Friday ladies", Brian smiled.

Ivy and Martha always came in after Market Day in the town. They had a stall in the pannier market, fresh vegetables, jams and superb pies.

Ivy beamed. "Yes, and a good day too. Sold the lot. Lots of visitors about, spending cash and needing to eat".

Martha, the largest of the two by some three stones beamed equally happily all round. "Ten years us have been in the market today, ten years exact".

"Then it's drinks on the house to celebrate Ladies, you deserve it" Brian grinned.

"Lovely boy", beamed Martha, "Brandy and Lovage's then please".

"You like the herb Lovage then ladies". I said.

"Well if it is laced with brandy then tis ansome, a bit special my dear" she grinned happily at me.

"Where do we get Lovage from then Tree? Don't see it round these parts I reckon", Bert enquired.

"I've seen it more in Scotland where they call it sea parsley and used to eat it as a vegetable. It is vivid green and rather like the Alexanders we see all along the roadsides here, that big creamy cow parsley like plant. It was used against cystitis too, and helps the appetite and digestion". Natural history was my subject and I loved every opportunity to further the cause.

"Oh well! Then 'tis certainly the stuff for me." Ivy interjected. All the more reason to drink it".

"Certainly is", I said. And it's excellent for flavouring meat dishes and soups as well as being used in perfumes".

"Tis a lovely smell I agree, all musky like". Said Martha her nose in her glass dreamily sniffing.

Ivy sipped hers reflectively. "Oh yes 'tis medicinal sure enough.

I feel very well. I could listen to you going on about how good these drinks are for us all night Tree. Makes it fair criminal to pass the inn door and not come in".

Brian raised the bottle towards them. "Good for trade too and good luck to you both for the next ten years".

8

Ted

The hedgebanks were rich in wildflowers, red campion, foxgloves, cow parsley, rosebay willowherb, dandelions, a veritable tapestry of colour interwoven with sounds and scents as bees and hoverflies went about their business. A yellowhammer sang from its perch but I could not agree with its sentiments. 'A little bit of bread and no cheese'. Makes for a poor ploughman's lunch I felt as I ambled down the road at a pace calculated to reach the inn door at noon time.

It was beautifully hot, the perfect summer day and I was blissfully aware of every flower's scent, birdsong and butterfly along the way.

The squeal of heavily applied bicycle brakes startled me from my reverie as a larger than life figure slewed sideways to skid to a halt before me.

"Hello Tree, been hoping to bump into you". It was Ted Cooke a bachelor of the parish, grinning from ear to ear at my deliberately exaggerated dive for the hedgebank and safety.

"You came pretty close to doing it too". I replied.

Ted laughed. For such a large man his laugh was shrill, about two octaves higher than his voice. He lived alone in the cottage where he was born, his parents having departed this life some ten years past. Ted had never married, his philosophy being that a man should learn to be happy on his own.

Enjoy your own company, why inflict it on others, he reckoned. And Ted was indeed always in a good mood.

"What can I do for you Ted?" I enquired as he sat upon his ancient black iron steed mopping his brow with a red and white spotted handkerchief.

"I made you a couple of nestboxes for your birds Tree, only I haven't seen you about so I rested them up on the hedge in my garden and do you know, a pair of coal tits nested in one of them. Wonderful it was." Ted beamed joyfully.

"Wonderful indeed." I exclaimed. "You should put some up in your garden trees then and see what comes next year".

"Aye, I'll do that. I was fair taken with the whole thing and all the babes flew one morning. Here, I've got notes on it for you".

Ted drew a wodge of folded papers from a pocket in his large grey tweed jacket. I scanned through the notes in delighted surprise, masses of notes on the nesting, even to exact times of day of each observation.

"Goodness Ted, this is perfect. I'll put all this on to Nest Record Cards for you to send to the British Trust for Ornithology".

Ted beamed delightedly. "I enjoyed every minute of it. Like having my own family in the garden. Fact is 'twas one of the nicest months of May I've known what with all that going on and in a box I had made myself".

"Yes it's a bit special Ted, especially when the young have fledged safely.

We wandered down the hill to the inn together where we quenched our thirsts with orange juices. Ted was a strict teeto-taller and virtually self sufficient with his fine garden vegeta-bles but he often came to the inn for a soft drink and chat with the locals.

"Here's to the day Ted". I raised my glass.

"Aye, to the day. Yer those pasties smell good. Let's be having one shall we. I love smells. Wouldn't want my nose to go deaf".

A deaf nose. What is the word for such I pondered. Blindness and deafness, but what of noses?

I ordered pasties for both of us.

"Good things pasties, dependable." Ted said.

"Dependable? How do you mean, Ted?"

He eyed me up and down. "Like your drill shirt and cord trousers. You know exactly what you've bought, dependable. I think pasties are the same. If I'm out for a meal I'll have two fried eggs rather than scrambled eggs. I love scrambled eggs at home if I do them myself cos I know what I've got. I know I've got two. Dependable see?"

Our food arrived, June the barmaid smiling sunnily as ever.

"What would you be if your nose didn't work June?" I asked her.

"Unhappy I expect, unless it was muck spreading time in the fields". She wandered off grinning.

Ted looked at me and shrugged. "Here, I'm going to do a spot of fishing tomorrow. Some lovely trout in the river. Can you get away and join me?"

"Where do you fish. I may wander along the riverbank to see what's about. Some dippers down along the river."

"I fish down below your place in the pool under Parsonage. Your bit's a mite fast. The solicitor from the big house often fishes along there with his doctor friend. A good flyman. He told me he once had a friend come into his surgery early in the day to weigh a fish on his scales. As the chap was leaving the waiting room was filling up and they all looked at this chap with the fish a bit odd like. Old doc Martin said to him, now give him the cod liver oil twice a day and let me know if he gets better. He said the patients faces were a picture."

We tucked into our country repast to the sound of blackbird song from a male whose mate was sitting on eggs just opposite the inn door in a dense hawthorn by a gateway.

Later Ted sat back and sighed contentedly. "That was good. Tis a pleasant world if you live a simple life. By the way did you know I've got a double?"

I looked at him somewhat surprised. Ted is around 6ft 3ins and big with it. His weather beaten face and greying full side-burns give him an almost unique look. John Wayne on a bicycle almost.

"Er double, Ted? No I didn't know".

"Oh aye. But I've never seen him myself. Every two weeks I gets into town to pick up bits and pieces. Brian here often gives me a lift. Well I always goes into the same shop for my pipe baccy and this woman who serves me keeps calling me Mr Stephens. Well last time I went in I told her I wasn't Mr Stephens, I am called Cooke and always have been. She stared at me and said she was sorry then told me I'd got a double.

Two weeks later I went in for my usual and she said, "Hello Mr Stephens, a chap called Cooke comes in here regular and he's the image of you"

Ted laughed. "Maze as a brish, she is".

It was an old phrase often heard when I was younger and we chatted for a while about local dialect. Then I recalled an old woman who lived over in the next village, Meg we all knew her as so I asked Ted what had happened to her in recent years as I had heard no word of her at all.

"Old Meg passed on about three years past. Wasn't ill or anything. Found her sat in her armchair with her little black and white TV on, the Baker did. In fact he took in her usual weekly order and was chatting to her about the programme until he realised she wasn't answering".

I had not been aware that Meg had died. She was a true eccentric and wise woman, not one of those who set themselves up to be eccentric and she had taught me a fair bit about the hedgerow herbs years ago. She was a white witch and proud of it, a bit persecuted by some who should have known better but such are often attacked for their beliefs no matter how much good they do. I said as much to Ted.

He stared at me long and hard. "If you liked her Tree then you knew the real person she was, as wise as they come and a lot of people round here have a lot to thank her for today for she healed many. She helped my old mother through her last year I can tell you. She were a good woman was Meg, rest her soul".

"I agree Ted, and she had a dignity about her and immense natural knowledge".

Ted sighed. "Aye that she did. I'll tell you a funny story. A gipsy woman called on Meg to sell clothes pegs and lace. She said she would read Meg's hand but Meg refused. Then she told the gipsy someone close to her was having a passionate affair with a dark stranger. The gipsy woman laughed but as she turned to leave Meg's doorstep she saw the mongrel bitch she had with her was mounted by a black labrador from the cottage up the road."

Ted's high pitched laughter echoed across the countryside.

9

Summer Days

One fine summer night young Donald came bursting into the bar where half a dozen of us were cooling off from the heat of the day. Donald was the local Don Juan in his self styled way and had moved from the Midlands with his parents to commute from village to town industrial estate each day. The smell of after-shave hit us from ten paces. I like cologne but this was the spicy limit.

"Hello chaps, any women in?" he called cheerfully.

Old George chuckled from his usual seat at the end of the bar." Got eye trouble then lad?" He asked.

"Eye trouble. Oh, I see. No I meant in tonight. I meant to be here earlier."

"You're dressed to kill I'll say that Don". I murmured.

Donald preened. He was wearing pristine white shorts and a shirt of violent royal blue with trainers to match.

"Been playing football then Don?" Asked Roger who was a local dealer in antiques and kept a few sheep on a small holding.

"Er, no just thought I'd wear something trendy. Got to be with it you know".

"Talking of being with it weren't you s'posed to be meeting a young lady at seven o'clock down by the stores tonight. I heard you telling the postman about it s'mornin". George stared hard at Donald who went a deep shade of red that did little for the shirt colour.

"Well yes that's right. I was there at seven and stood about til eight and gone but she didn't turn up. Well I wasn't having that was I, so I stood her up".

George looked at me and burst out laughing. At that moment two young women did come into the bar, smartly dressed town girls out for the night and dressed up to the nines.

Donald breezed over to them immediately, oozing confidence and after shave.

"Evening ladies. Can I buy you a drink just to be friendly like?"

The girls eyed him up and down coolly.

"Been playing football then?" one asked. Roger and George bleated with poorly stifled laughter.

Don was cool under fire. "You like shorts then do you?" he grinned posing against the bar.

The taller of the girls smiled sweetly. "Yeah, we love shorts. We'll have a large gin and tonic each and thanks very much".

We all turned to the bar. Donald had met his match and it was going to be an expensive evening for him.

"Lord knows times are a changing too fast for me Tree" George said. "I was down at the fete last Saturday in a queue for a cuppa and I said to this person beside me, now look at that teenager in the pink jeans, the long hair and sunglasses, is that a girl or a boy? She's a girl, and she's my daughter, was the annoyed reply. Well, I turned and apologised, saying I didn't mean to be rude and hadn't realised he was her father. Cor was I ever wrong. The 'chap' was his mother and told me so in no uncertain terms, storming off in a huge black trouser suit and heavy boots just like I wears to church on Sundays I swear".

As often with George's yarns there was no answer.

Alec, Children & Things

Warm sunshine, a blue sky filled with white wispy clouds as if mirroring the sheep in the fields opposite our Beer Garden bench where Alec Avery and I sat enjoying a well earned ploughmans. It being summertime the inn was well frequented with visitors to the nearby National Trust property or en route to the coast a few miles away.

I quaffed my glass pool of the dark liquid that cuts away the dust and thirst from the weary travellers throat, a Mackeson.

Alec was eating silently and then he leaned back on the rustic seat and sighed contentedly to the world at large.

"Good to have my car back again. Cost me £100 to have her jigged out and repaired". He pushed his knife blade into a piece of thick cheddar, dipped it into some Branston pickle and chewed happily.

I asked him what had happened to his vehicle, an old green Jaguar which he kept highly polished and running smoothly, a bit like Alec himself for he was a long, rangey fellow who always looked smart in dark shirts with light woollen ties and cream trousers, and a flat cap worn to the back of his head as if it followed him around.

"Well, it didn't happen to me exactly. Happened to my wife. She backed out of the garage a bit smartish like, hit the garage door, ran over the lads bike, straight across the lawn in reverse, tore up all the roses and the box hedge, out into the road and then she lost control of the car".

"Oh, not 'til then?" I couldn't prevent a chuckle.

"Twad'n funny Tree. Darn good job the vicar's wife was driving down the road. My wife hit her car and that stopped her going into the opposite hedge". He looked at me seriously.

"Why a 'good job' she hit the other car? Surely that was bad?"

I asked him.

"No, not really. Vicar's wife drives slow. Think what would have happened if she'd hit a fast driver".

I took another mouthful of my drink, contemplating his point of view. I had a strange feeling it was going to be one of those funny peculiar days when sense does not always make sense. We finished our meals in silent appreciation of wholesome fare.

June came past precariously carrying a tray loaded with drinks and food. She set it down before a couple of holiday-makers and came over to say hello.

"How are you June" I smiled a greeting as Alec raised his glass to her.

"I'm fine Tree. Got a ticking off this morning though for being late. Madam is in a difficult mood". She nodded in the direction of the interior.

"How late?" Enquired Alec.

"Oh, over twenty minutes". She saw we were grinning. "Well, I try getting in on time but it makes such a long day". She wiggled away smiling.

Just then there was a horrified squeal from the next table. We looked to see that one of the large flock of rooks that had just flown over had scored a direct hit on the shoulder of a smart looking woman's obviously expensive blouse. The raucous cries of the departing birds expressed well their lack of concern I thought.

Alec called out. "Now ma'am that really was a bit of good luck".

The woman glared across at us. "You don't really believe that superstitious rubbish in this day and age do you?"

Alec smiled. Definitely ma'am. That lot could have gone straight in your drink".

"Oh, awful place the countryside, awful bird". She jumped up to disappear to make repairs. The man with her was grinning into his soup.

We rose, calling our goodbyes to June and each other, Alec going across to the car park as I strode back up the road in the heat of a perfect afternoon. Passing Lilac Cottage I heard the sound of woodworking activity and stopping to glance over the hedge saw a lad of around 14 years planing away at an old plank. He was giving it all he had, watched by a blonde pig-tailed young girl of 10 or so, as delightful a picture of young country life as one could imagine, the two youngsters backed by a hedge bank of foxgloves in full flower.

I went onward, thinking no more of the matter until some two hours later when I was strolling back from my work and could hear the same sound issuing from the garden. The girl was now sitting in the gateway drinking a tall glass of lemonade, the boy still planing the plank and looking hot but happy as he toiled.

"Whatever is he making?" I had to ask.

The girl smiled sweetly. "Guess" She said.

"Well he's been at it for at least two hours so it must be very useful". I countered.

"Yes. It is useful and he is doing it for me".

I took another look but the boy, hearing voices, came over to the gate.

"That's enough now Susie, I'm boiling hot. Your old rabbit".

That was the clue I needed. I seized it.

"Ah a rabbit hutch. You're making your sister a rabbit hutch.

The boy looked at me puzzled as he picked up a glass of lemonade poured by his grinning sister. He pointed across the garden to where a fine rabbit hutch stood under the hedge and I could now see a large black rabbit munching away in its own compound beneath an apple tree.

"Mmmm? Then are you making the rabbit a playpen?"

"Playpen. He plays about in the garden". He stared at me as if I'd just landed from Mars.

"Er, well then, what?" I said lost for ideas.

The girl giggled as the boy looked at me patiently.

I'm planing down the old wood cos we've run out of wood shavings for the rabbit to bed down in and we cant get into town until next week".

"Of course. That's wonderful." I assented and waved goodbye as I strolled off down the steep hill knowing that to miss the obvious usually proves ones undoing.

It was indeed one of those funny old days. As I turned the next bend in the road Harold Beck crossed in front of me pulling a motor lawn mower and sporting a huge smile. He waited for me, mopping his brow as I told him it looked as if he was going to be busy for the weekend.

"Just borrowed Frank's mower. A brainwave," he smiled mentioning his neighbour.

"Yours broken then?" I enquired.

"Come and have a cup of tea", Harold parried, ushering me jovially through the honeysuckle covered arched gateway leading into a large lawned garden. We strolled along a crazy paving pathway chatting about the immaculate garden as we went.

"Your garden looks superb" I said in praise of his work and then as we gazed about, "but your lawn is perfect!"

Harold was chuckling away obviously well pleased as his wife appeared with a tray of tea and biscuits. We sat at a table beneath two Bramley apple trees as Angela poured and handed me a cup of tea.

"Strong and with one sugar Tree." She remembered from many happy chats over the years. I sipped and stared at the two of them. They were alike, some 10 years younger than I with healthy country complexions and that dark hair that never seems to grey in some people.

"Don't tell me you are going in for mowing lawns and gardening for others? Not at your age surely?" I eyed them quizzically.

"Blunt as ever Tree, you beggar. But no, I agree we're too old for that sort of thing". He smiled and sipped his tea.

"Put him out of his misery Harry." Angela said giggling.

"Right. Now then Tree, I know you're a man of your word so this is between you, us and the gatepost mind".

"Enough said." I agreed intrigued.

"Well now, 'tis Friday you see. I've borrowed the mower until Monday, from Frank's missus while he's at work." He paused, taking a great gulp from his heavily sugared cup.

This weekend we are all going to sleep late, in peace, even Frank's missus.

You see, Frank cuts his cussed great lawns from first light every Saturday out front, and the cussed great back lawns every Sunday. Fair drives us mad. Now he's had his chips." Harold rocked on his chair in great glee.

"Have another cup Tree." Angela said.

I nodded. It was indeed peaceful. The goldfinches, too, would have a peaceful time and Frank himself would surely benefit from the change.

11

Ben, Mary & All...

One summer night Ben Tanton and I were discussing the local wildlife. Ben was a farm worker who well remembered the times when he wandered the countryside with his father or one or two friends on days when quail were to be seen each summer and corncrakes might call from the fields before harvesting time. They would expect to hear an otter whistle from the river of an evening, as much a sound of the countryside as the church bells and crowing cockerels.

"Cocks not allowed to crow in some parts you know Tree, get taken to bleddy Court if they makes a noise and wakes up these yuppie types. Don't know what it's coming to, they'll want to muzzle the birds in summer next". Ben was rightly angry about such people who really ought not to live in the countryside if they have to play God and try to change it.

We had been leaning on the bar chatting about birds of prey when I suddenly realised I had been going on at length about two pairs of close nesting sparrowhawks and the sheer delight of my observations in a nearby wood for rather a long while.

This was brought home to me by June the barmaid who leaned across the bar and said meaningfully to Ben that I would get more out of ten minutes watching sparrowhawks than from a night out with a good woman.

"Oh, I dunno", Ben said, we all know what these naturists are like."

There was a roar of laughter from around the bar but undeterred by his error, which suggested I wandered around wearing less than a loincloth, Ben said, "Anyway, what would ee want out with a good woman".

Ben was a lovely man, a real character with a way of delivering some amazing remarks then creating great silent moments, like Exmoor tarns into which remarks would be tossed as water-smoothed pebbles to create a few ripples then vanish forever.

Once he said to me, " you know what Tree, I just talk the way I think but more often".

Yet was Ben more of a thinker than he pretended? Most people are. Twas not so long ago that he gazed at the barmaid contemplatively for some while, sipping slowly at his pint, then nudging me he said, "You know what Tree, June is the most opposite of the opposite sex I've ever seen".

A compliment and a half methinks.

Once a holidaymaker who had been chatting to Ben about the area for well over an hour told him he must have the most amazing memory, asking how he had contrived to learn so much.

"Laziness, just laziness", Ben replied. "I hear bits here and I hear bits there and I'm just too lazy to forget it".

Perhaps one of his most picturesque sayings, at least that I recall, was when a woman eating a pasty had half of it fall into her lap.

As she carefully cleared up the mess Ben sighed and said, "Now there's a lady who is a mite lap-hazard in her eating".

Mary

Mary is a farmer's wife who for years has filled one of the farmhouse windows with produce for sale to anyone who cared to call and buy.

"SPUDS HERE." Reads a sign on a large white painted board beside the gateway to the farmhouse, indeed I feel sure people know the farm better as 'Spudshere' than by its real name burned into a piece of elm next to the board.

Mary is a lovely lady of some 60 years young and as jolly as they come. She had never been out of Devon in her life, had had two holidays and was always glad to get back home. They'd gone to South Devon and reckoned it was far enough. As she was always fond of telling anyone, there's nowhere prettier than around home anyway.

On a day of sunshine and showers she screeched to a halt beside me along the road to the Sanctuary in the battered pick-up they had used for several years.

"Got some campers in top field this week. I've told em to keep well off your patch Tree. I know the deer are in there again, saw eight or ten yesterday".

"Thanks Mary I appreciate that", I replied. "And how goes it with you and the family?"

"Oh much the same as ever. I sold one of the campers a dozen eggs and a load of spuds a couple of days ago and off he went in his car. Only two fields from the farm and he wouldn't use shanks pony. Anyway he came back an hour later saying the eggs was broke cos I'd put em under the spuds in the carrier bag. Well I soon told him you puts em at the bottom so that when they break they don't run over everything else in the bag. Thought that was common sense I told him. As for my old man he's as daft as they are. We had this French couple staying in a tent last week and they could hardly speak any English. Proper furriners they was and I said to Jack I couldn't understand a word they said.

Jack said did I remember those Frenchie films with those sub-title things on the bottom of the screen. He said when those campers speak look down at their feet and you'll see what they'm saying. Silly old gawk."

"How's Janet these days Mary?" I asked. Janet is their only daughter, wed to an airman and 'gone the whole way to Scotland to live.' Mary once told me.

"Oh she's fine. They've been trying for a baby for three years now and she's pregnant at last. Always knew she had it in her".

"For that gem you deserve a glass of stout Mary" I said. "I'm off to the inn right now."

"Good. I think Jack's meeting Roger down there about now anyway, sorting out some poultry business. I could do with a freshener.

She drove us on down the hill to the inn, timed to perfection as Jack and Roger were just wandering in ahead of us. The inn was gradually filling with people from the car park, two couples already eating at tables, the smell of mushroom soup and hot pies deliciously wafting on the air along with the sound of Billie Jo Spears laying yet another 'Blanket On The Ground'.

Jack looked up from ordering and grinned when he saw us beside him at the Bar. "Cor Mary, now I know what you gets up to when I'm out working. Usual both?"

Mary laughed." Well Jack if they'm going to gossip about me in here with Tree then I'd start worrying seeing as how you came in with Roger".

Jack guffawed. "Cor look at that chap on the one-armed bandit.", he said.

At the gaming machine against the wall by the pool room a young man dressed in black denim was playing with flair, posing for all and sundry to see, doing his best to read the machine's mind. One second he would yank the handle down fair fit to break it off, another he would caress it then gently pull as if to tease the money out. Then he stood back beckoning with all fingers working, only to dive in again, looking greatly puzzled when the machine did not comply. Olivier and Gielgud here is thy successor I thought.

His girl companion, dressed in lurid lime green blouse and burnt orange jeans began to smooch him amorously. Nature had obviously not pleased her for she was heavily made up with an imitation orange tan and bright green eye shadow, her hair wonderful to observe, a morass of psychadelic colours skilfully chosen for their incompatibility.

I looked down at my sombre hues of dark green and brown. God, how boring I am, I thought.

Mary brought me out of my reverie of reflection, tut-tutting as the couple embraced even more deeply.

"Didn't do that in my day. Least ways not in public" she confided. Kept it private in our day didn't we Jack?" she smiled at him.

"Aye. Cor, for a public display like that I'd sell tickets and make a bob or two". Jack grinned back at his wife.

I thought about her comment; 'twas true. The 50s and 60s had changed things to the extent that exhibitionists were ten a penny these days. Freedom it is called but it isn't freedom, just a rebellious phase that smacks at self discipline. It will be a cyclical thing probably, another 20 years and niceness will take the place of aggression once again. If we are still here 20 years from now...

Again Mary's voice broke in on my musing.

"I'm broad minded but they've got consciences made of elastic these days Tree."

Consciences of elastic. We've all had them at times I suppose.

There was a rattling and banging from the machine, cheers from the young couple.

"Cor, now he's hit the jackpot as well." Jack muttered.

We clinked glasses. "To the young." We toasted.

"Aye", said Roger. "Tis a hard enough life for them these days even if life is also easier. At least we could all find jobs years ago, even change them as and when we wanted.

Jack's brothers, Ted and Don joined us smelling of fresh air and haymaking, and in need of liquid refreshment. Don patted me on the back in his hearty way, which almost sent me on into the pool room. Ted gazed at the blissful young couple now sitting holding hands at the bar.

"Who was it who said today's lamented modern ways will be tomorrow's good old days?"

"You just did Ted." I answered. "Tell me, you have been a bachelor all your life, why did you never get married?"

"Oh I aint been a bachelor all my life yet Tree. But I'd rather go through life wanting summat I never had than having summat I didn't want, wouldn't you agree?"

There was no argument to that. Jack joined in asking about the birdlife in the area as he had not seen anything like the numbers of birds he used to when farming with his father years ago. We chatted about declines, about the flail mowing of hedges as an example, and the constant silage cuts and pollution, all factors in the quite obvious decrease in wildlife.

"All down to money, flailed hedges. Can't afford time or money to steep them these days. 'Steep' is a country term for layering, the best way to maintain a good hedge.

"Talking of birds tell Tree about that green budgie Jack," interjected Mary.

"Oh he don't want to know about that" Jack replied looking a trifle embarrassed.

"Well I'll tell it as it was then." Mary chuckled as the others looked resignedly skywards.

Mary settled back and unwove the tale of Sprout the green budgie who had arrived unbidden in their garden, caught in a fruit cage, which kept winged marauders from the fruiting treasures Jack so lovingly grew and nurtured.

"We had an old birdcage in the barn so Jack caught the bird and put it in that. He was really taken with it and spent hours trying to get it to talk. They used to chirp at each other like a couple of old fools." Mary laughed.

"It wasn't that bad Mary", Jack protested but he was grinning, trying to steer around the meat of the story I felt sure.

Mary was undeterred. "Go home with ee Jack, couple of old chatterboxes you were. Anyway one night I woke up and I could hear Sprout chattering right there in the room or so it seemed yet the bird was downstairs fast asleep in his cage when I went to look. Next morning Jack said I was dreaming about the bird but it happened again the next night and still Sprout was in his cage asleep. Well I can tell ee I was fair fed up having these dreams so the next night I sat up reading my 'People's Friend' magazine and there 'twas again ever so loud.

Do you know, there was Jack lying asleep, chirping away exactly like that little bird. The budgie had taught Jack to talk instead of t'other way round". Mary roared with laughter.

"Worse still," Jack chuckled, "we didn't get a word of English out of that bird in the five years we had him, but he was a lovely little chap".

Ted was grinning widely as he stared over our heads at the beam over the bar. On it were pinned many business cards, taxi phone numbers and sundry services that may at some time be useful to the customers at the inn.

"Look at that'n." Ted pointed.

Someone from the area called Susie had written, 'Lift to Barnstaple wanted 3 days a week, desperate'. Neatly written beneath were the words 'how desperate?'...

13

Old Jan

"Dear old Jan. Tis real sad he passed away Bill".

"Aye. The place wont be the same without old Jan".

I pricked up my ears. Old Jan? Though I did not reside in the village I knew most of the locals and could not recall an old Jan. Obviously he was well liked to cause old Bill Trebble and Dan Blackmore to express such concern.

I caught Bill's eye. "Old Jan? Died then?"

"Yes lad. Last Saturday. Dropped down in his own orchard like he was pole-axed. Dan here saw it happen".

"Oh dear, bit of a shock then, heart was it?" I asked.

"Aye. Gave out it did, but not unexpected like". Bill sipped at his glass of best bitter and shook his head resignedly.

"Getting on a bit then was he?" I asked desperately trying to recall Jan to mind.

"Thirty years. Almost to the day." Dan answered my question. "One of the saddest moments I'll ever see".

"Thirty years!" I exploded. Then more reverently, "and you say not unexpected?" It was no wonder I could not call Jan to mind for I had been going over the older villagers in my mind. "He must have been quite ill then, how awful".

"Aye 'twas awful lad. But he never had a days illness that I can recall" Mind you he had a heavy fall last winter come to think of it. Went down a cropper on the ice but he seemed alright afterwards".

"What was his surname then Bill?" I asked.

"Surname? What do you mean surname lad?" He looked at me puzzled.

"Well, second name, family name, you know".

"Oh I see." Bill stared at Daniel as if I'd had too much to drink. "Stephens. You know, up by the mill where the orchard joins the road. They've lived there for years".

I could see the property clearly now in my mind's eye but I did not know the family that well. "Yes of course. Where the old brown horse always looks out over the gate. I've never met the tenants".

"Aye lad. Only he wont look out over the gate again, not Old Jan. Wont be the same without him around".

14

Summer Nights

Bill is Chairman of the Parish Council and quite rightly takes the position seriously. "Quite a meeting this evening." He said as we strolled into the garden area of the inn where wooden seats and tables invited the outdoor lovers to remain in the sunshine. "Took all of half an hour. One of those planning matters that we in the village all agree with but the District Council will find some awkward reason to object to as usual".

"Nothing simple about planning matters Bill. Or if they are simple they have to be made to look complicated".

"Simple? Tis the planners who are simple sometimes. They should get rid of District Councils and just have Parish Councils. Let the people who know the places get on with the job."

I sat outside facing the roadway with a pleasant view of fields opposite as Bill wandered off for a Tomato Juice. He came back with his glass and apologised for not asking what I might want.

"I've a flask of coffee actually Bill. I wasn't coming in here until we met up but I may just get away with it." Even as I poured so Hazel the landlady appeared in the garden with eyes like a hawk.

"Tree! You can't sit here drinking your own coffee you know. Come along now you cheeky thing".

I thought fast for others in the Beer Garden were watching and now aware of my misdemeanour. "Sorry Hazel. A Jack Daniels please." I said.

"Sorry Tree, we don't keep that in as yet." Hazel grimaced.

"Mmm. A Glenlivet then if you will".

"Don't have that particular one either." She said eyeing me suspiciously.

"Then a Glenmorangie, you must have that." I smiled.

"No, we don't!" She said sharply.

"They don't seem to have anything you want do they Tree," grinned Bill realising my game.

"Oh well, drink your coffee this time. We'll get in a bigger selection of spirits eventually". Hazel wandered off.

Bill chuckled and asked how things were going. We chatted about our respective work, enjoying the fresh air. He told me how he had begun carpentry classes at a local Community College in readiness for his retirement and how on enrolment night the class tutor had asked his age saying that pensioners receive a concessionary fee.

"I told her I was 67 and did she need proof. She told me, no, so I says to her do I look honest then my dear. No, she told me, you look 67".

We were chuckling when Ron Facey arrived in the carpark in his large red Ford Estate car, which he drove aggressively. Seeing us in the garden he came across, heaving his bulk into the seat opposite us and waving to June who acknowledged she knew his tipple.

A large boned. untidy man he had a way of needling people if they were inclined to bite. It seemed he just had to, insecurity perhaps or some inner enjoyment.

"Lo Bill, lo Tree, nort better to do then Tree?" An opening gambit he often used.

"Evening Ron, how's your wife these days" I countered ignoring the query as to whether I had ought better to do.

"Compared to what?" was Ron's reply. I felt I had heard that before somewhere.

Strange characters these. I knew a fellow in the town always ready to dart in with some barbed comment or other. The same chap would write letters to the local paper under a pseudonym, picking away at local matters. Putting pen to paper would not be Ron's cup of tea though, just the stirring bit , yet his house and garden were quite superbly looked after and one of the best kept in the area.

"Quite a hot day today Ron". Again I ignored his own comment.

"Aye tis. Thermometer in the greenhouse showed 30 degrees this afternoon so I poured water on it. Didn't want it that hot in there."

Ron's expression never changed. The couple sitting next to us stared and nudged each other and whispered. They looked like holidaymakers, tourists, or grockles depending how one saw tourism as a boon or bane for the area.

Ron stared at them closely. "On your holidays then folks?" he asked bluntly.

The couple looked at him and smiled, perhaps pleased he seemed quite human after all.

"Yes." The man said "We honeymooned in the Exmoor area when we married 20 years ago so we are back to enjoy it all over again, lovely place".

Ron did not reply but continued to stare in his usual manner.

The man continued. "We are from Dorset, Hardy country, place called Chettle, Cranborne Chase way, know it?"

The best I could do was say I knew Cranborne Chase from visiting the Badbury Rings. The couple warmed to the chat, talking about their two children, their cottage and the Dorset countryside. The man then told us they had had a stay-at-home holiday last year.

"Oh, broke then were you?" immediately came from Ron.

Bill looked at me. I rose. "Can I buy you a drink, this flask coffee has lost its flavour, pint of Poachers Bill?"

Ron rose quickly. "Not for me. Got to get on to the garden this evening".

The Dorset woman looked at him with the sweetest of smiles.

"What a quaint idea." She said. "We use artificial fertiliser back home"

Ron stared at her. The usually expressionless face twitched. Then came the great braying laugh that is rarely heard in the village.

"You've got a good'n there chap alright. Night then all", and he was away across the road still braying his laughter into the summer's night.

15

Dog & Fox Evening

"Children." Jack Snell mumbled. "Last December I said to this ten year old lad who lives next door, take my Christmas cards and deliver them to save me the postage and you will get 5p each for delivering them. You can spend that on presents. Well off ee went and when ee came back ee had three cards in his hand. Ee said 14 of the people paid up, 4 said they'd got enough Christmas cards and 3 others said 2p was plenty enough to pay. Silly little chap".

We were leaning on the gate opposite the inn entrance, glasses in hand enjoying the view and the fresh air, chatting about anything and nothing. There was Jack and his dog Ben, Steve the Inn pool captain and myself. Ben was sitting quietly watching every movement in the fields beyond, tongue lolling, panting as dogs do on hot days.

"Got too much money today kids have" Steve said. He was only around 18 himself and we grinned at his knowing words. He went on, "only thing you can get a kid to do for a few pence these days is toss you for it".

"Words of wisdom." Jack said, "and to get them doing owt for nowt as they say is pretty nigh impossible. My son asked little Jamie to wash the car last week and he asked his dad what he'd pay him to do it. Worth a clip round the ear in my day that was."

"Fancy a game of pool anyone" Steve asked us hopefully.

Jack looked at him. "No thanks boy. Saw you playing last week. All bang and speed. I like a game of strategy and tactics like chess". Jack's reply spoke for both of us as I was more than content to stand and watch the evening leaning on the gate.

Steve snorted. "Strategy and tactics? What are they?"

Jack stared at him for long moments and I could almost

hear the well oiled wheels whirring in his sharp country brain. Then he said, "Well boy I saw ee taking young Sharon from top farm out last weekend didn't I?"

"Yes you did, what about it?" Steve looked puzzled.

"Well boy, when you chatted her up that was strategy. What you did when you took her out, that was tactics". Jack roared with laughter at the look on Steve's face, receiving an answering whinny from a horse in the next field. Steve wandered off into the inn seeking a pool victim.

The vicar joined us, walking his newly acquired dog though it always seemed to have the vicar in tow, a puller of a corgi it was, always on a taut leash.

"You ought to get a harness for that dog vicar, better than a dog collar." Jack suggested.

I spluttered into my Mackeson as the vicar smiled.

"A dog collar has done me alright for 30 years Jack so it will have to do for the dog" he smiled benignly.

"Yer that would have been a good joke if I'd intended it vicar", Jack chuckled. Ben growled a warning as the vicar's dog investigated him too closely.

"Busy then vicar?" I asked him.

"Not today actually. I've been listening to a bit of Shakespeare on the radio actually" he answered.

Jack looked scornful. "Huh! You know what they say about Shakespeare. Nobody would have heard of him if he hadn't written all those plays".

The vicar smiled and shook his head then left at some speed as the corgi spied a cat crossing the road below the inn. "Byeeee!" he called back along the road as the two sped around the bend.

Jack nudged me, telling Ben to 'stay' and I saw a fox crossing the field before us with a red chicken clamped firmly in his jaws. I was sure from the shape of his head it was a dog fox, the golden evening light shining on his fur.

"Proud little devil, look at him go. That's one of the Rhode Island Reds from the manor I'll wager." Jack's voice tailed off as we watched the fox move up along the hedgerow his coat glowing in the sunset light as he trotted through the high buttercups taller than he to disappear into a bramble brake against the hedge.

Ben was alert, hackles up but obedient to Jack's command to stay.

"Now that was a sight for a summers evening Jack". I said.

"Aye. Twas but they'll have to take better care of their chickens up at the house".

I looked closely at him as he spoke and he read my thoughts.

"No, I shan't say a word Tree. Let'n be I say. There's a few about but the countryside can afford them".

We watched the fields for a while in silence. The setting sun touched golden shimmers to the treetops, the foliage turning from green to almost black, gradually vanishing into shadows as the light faded. Pale moths frolicked and somewhere a tawny owl hooted its welcome to the night.

"Are you coming inside Tree, 'tis getting a mite chilly?" Jack asked.

"No. I'm on my way Jack. The fox was the perfect end to a lovely evening. Thanks for the chat. See you next week perhaps".

"Night Tree, go safe boy", and Jack was gone into the noise and light of the inn which vanished with the closing of the door.

16

Autumn Days

Summer had drifted rather lazily into autumn, the swallows, martins and swifts moving on to warmer climes. I had heard stags roaring in the woods beyond my Sanctuary for it was the time of the rut. Anytime now the clocks would alter, rendering the evenings darker. The first hint of frost was on the air as I reached the inn, the scent of chimney smoke from a log fire welcoming. I had brought a painting of badgers, a sort of commission from the professor, and having left him was wandering down the road enjoying the nip of frost on my nose and waving back to the woman cottager who lived next to the inn. The sound of a car horn came loud on the frosty air as Denis Cole and his lovely wife Jill pulled into the car park in their Land Rover, waving and smiling. I waited, holding the door open for them to precede me in and asked them what they were drinking.

"Beer and crisps for us both." Jill smiled. And thanks, and we haven't seen you in ages, where have you been keeping yourself?"

We chatted over our various recent happenings and then George, in his usual seat, bar-propping, joined the conversation.

"Ah, listen to this folks" he sighed, holding a printed pamphlet close to his horn-rimmed glasses. "She has creamy flesh, shallow eyes, peels easily and is readily available. What do you make of that then?"

"She sounds friendly she does" Jill chuckled.

George looked at us over his spectacles. "She's a new variety of potato. I might go back to gardening again. Better than those feathered birds of yours Tree." He grinned broadly.

173

Denis said, "Now tell him about that swan then Tree, the one Jill likes so much". He looked at me expectantly. So I obliged.
"But now they drift on the still water,
Mysterious, beautiful, Among what rushes will they build?
By what lake's edge or pool, Delight men's eyes when I awake some day, to find they have flown away"... I raised my Mackeson.
"Barmy". George said.
"Lovely", said Jill, "and who wrote it?"
I tried to remember but I was better at recalling the words than the names of poets and writers.
"Yeats I thinks, or Keats. Somebody with an 'eats' anyway."
A couple came in and sat in the tall pew-like seat behind the door with their drinks. Then the door swung open again, a large shadow looming framed against the fading light. The figure took a step forward then slowly keeled over to lie prone,
The woman behind the door shrieked as her companion leapt up. Denis and I rushed over to the crumpled figure.
'It's old Cuthbert Down" Denis gasped as Brian the landlord joined us. We rolled Cuthbert onto his back, Brian opening the shirt collar. "We'd better get an ambulance quick" he grunted.
"Rather you got me a pint chaps". Cuthbert suddenly sprang upright bellowing with laughter. "I planned that one as I strolled down the road".
He laughed again then seeing the shocked couple behind the door he sheepishly told them it was one of his little practical jokes.
"You're daft Cuthbert!" Jill wagged a reproving finger at him.
"You will play these silly pranks all over the village." She said and Brian joined in ticking him off for scaring the lot of us.
Cuthbert chuckled. Go on, you know 'tis only my bit of fun. I could see there were only two or three cars in the carpark. I bet I cheered you up really".
"Well maybe you did when we thought you'd snuffed it you old twerp". Jill giggled. "You had us going there Cuthbert".
I looked at Cuthbert. He stood solid at around 5ft 10ins and some sixteen stones I guessed. A jovial red faced man with

dark gipsy eyes, I'd only met him a couple of times and he was always a joker.

Brian set a pint down before him. "Glad I didn't have to lift you Cuthbert you daft beggar," he smiled.

"Cheers." Cuthbert said, then sniffed warily at his drink. "Thought it might be cold tea" he said and quaffed half of the liquid down with a toss of his head.

"No," Brian replied, "'tis the slops from the other glasses".

Cuthbert stared. There was another but milder shriek from the woman behind the door.

"Its alright ma'am. Just my little joke this time" Brian assured her, going back to the crossword he and his wife raced each other for most days. We downed our respective refreshments.

"You silly old b......" George said to Cuthbert who smilingly went over to chat with him.

It was suddenly very peaceful in the bar, one of those rare moments afforded by country inns on week nights, a blackbird singing its last evensong from a roost in the hedgebank lit from the windows,

Brian's wife Hazel came into the bar, greeted everyone and put coins in the jukebox. The warm voice of Jim Reeves gently filled the room and she leaned with Brian to do the crossword.

"To send forth buds and shoots, seven letters". You should know that one Tree," she called.

"Bloom, with four Os." Denis said.

"Twerp" said Jill.

"Twerp is five letters" Hazel chuckled.

"Burgeon, try burgeon" I suggested.

"Burgeon? That's what caviare comes from." Cuthbert mumbled.

"That's sturgeon, the roe of a sturgeon", I said.

"I see the horoscope is on the same page", Jill said to Hazel.

"Always is. You can read yours later", replied Hazel who did not like having the crossword interrupted.

"You don't believe in that rubbish do you Jill?" George asked. "Why one day it told me to go out and make two new friends and see what happens. I was young and gullible then so I did. Nothing happened and I was stuck with two new friends.

Jill laughed." I always read them but only take notice if they are good".

"Ten letter word meaning to improve or make more endurable. Begins with 'A', fourth letter is an 'L', Hazel looked around at us all.

"Ameliorate", I suggested. I loved words.

"Lovely, gives me the 'T' that I want", Hazel smiled.

"Coo, just think, Dolly Parton could ameliorate my life" chuckled Denis.

"What was that?" Jill asked him.

"Oh nothing dear, nothing, " Denis said, winking at us.

"I wouldn't exactly call Dolly Parton nothing. She be a fine pair of females. Got a really lovely voice", Cuthbert added hastily as Hazel glared at him.

He looked at his watch. "Nearly ten. May as well get along folks. Usual for my missus please."

Brian handed him a bottle of Guinness.

George rose and I said I'd walk a ways with him. We left to a hail of farewells and Cuthbert shouting he would catch us up on his bike. Outside the frosty air was fresh and exhilarating, stars twinkling in a clear sky shared with a gibbus moon with a wide halo around her, the landscape silver and black and very beautiful.

"Drop of rain tomorrow George do you reckon?"

"Aye. The moon appears to think so Tree."

We walked down the hill in silence, enjoying the night and the hooting of a tawny owl from dark trees nearby. The sound of the inn door slamming reminded us of Cuthbert's farewell.

"That'll be Cuthbert about to walk home." George said.

"I think he'll ride down this hill don't you George, we'd best keep well in".

I had visions of the bulky Cuthbert zooming down the steep incline. "He's certainly fond of his japes. I fell for it tonight, hook, line and sinker." I chuckled.

George laughed. "He wins a few does Cuthbert, but I reckon he'll walk without this". He held up the front bicycle light from Cuthbert's trusty steed. "I'll leave it on his doorstep. He's fond of a joke is Cuthbert".

We strolled on smiling. In the distance the little hamlet was going to sleep, window by window.

17

Of Cars & Rain & Things

Charles was the only one 'in' the bar when I entered, flicking raindrops from my lightweight Barbour. "Bit damp out." I called as he turned towards me as immaculately dressed as ever in sports coat and flannels.

"Yes. Don't expect many in tonight, not in this weather. The forecast said fog and no rain in this area".

"Well the fog is running down the gutters Charles", I laughed, and, "Yes a Mackeson Brian if you will please".

Brian came over with my drink, nodding towards Charles, so I followed his gaze. Charles was moving his head up and down as he stared into the fireplace, in a strange bobbing fashion.

"Going to hire yourself out as one of those silly dogs people have bobbing their heads in the backs of cars then Charles?" I said.

"What. Oh no, sorry. I've got these new bi-focals. Fell over the step when I came in. Take some getting used to. It's like being in water half way up your eyeballs".

"Yes I know. I've worn specs since my 20s so I can sympathise" I told him.

"Had to laugh yesterday," said Brian. "Went into town and I was sitting in the car waiting for Hazel to come from the hairdressers when this woman arrives at the next car absolutely loaded with shopping. She put one bag on the bonnet and held on to another against her shoulder and chin while searching like mad for her keys. Ever the gentleman, and as it wasn't raining I get out and offer to hold her shopping. I stands there holding the parcels and bags while she finds the keys and unlocks the car door. I went to lean in with the shopping when we both bursts out laughing. Do you know it was a little MG with the soft-top roof right back. She could have put the shopping right onto the seat the whole time. Were our faces red."

"Mmmm." Muttered Charles. He didn't laugh much but it was a sign he was amused. A longer Mmmmmmm would show he was highly amused. Then he said, "Do you remember our new little car when I first bought it? I got home one frosty evening and put a blanket over the front. She started first time next morning so I was putting the blanket on the next night when my wife came out. She asked why was I doing that when the engine was in the rear. It was too."

"Lovely" Brian said. "It doesn't look as if anyone will be in tonight so how about us three having a pasty and drink on me".

As always the pasties tasted delicious, the more so on a chilly, rainy night. Charles eyed my glass.

"You don't drink much do you Tree. Always a Mackeson?"

"Yes, usually only the one actually. Good for you they say".

"I used to drink, really drink," Brian said. "But keeping a pub I don't bother now. I was in Germany in the Army. REME. Three of us used to play Russian roulette in the Beer Gardens at weekends".

"Good grief!" I exclaimed, having visions of a revolver being handed around with one bullet in it.

Brian chuckled. "We called it that. We drank schnapps. That's the stuff if you want to know what blind drunk means. We'd drink it for a couple of hours until the world was just a haze and then one of us would leave. The trick was for the other two to guess who had left."

"Mmmmmmm", murmured Charles.

18

Old George

Old George, or Garge as the locals knew him, had been the inn's mainstay during the years of its beginnings when the none too large selection of available drinks and the odd bag of crisps did not attract many customers. On the coldest winter nights when snow drove off Exmoor sideways or it rained in sheets Old George would be in 'His' place at the far end of the bar, on 'His' stool. There he would rest back against the huge stone pillar armed with pipe and whisky glass, seeing all. Few came to the inn without Old George knowing. He was as the beams and fireplace, part and parcel and one expected to see him there. If he wasn't then either he or his wife was ill.

Thus did George's regular glasses of Grouse help sustain the innkeepers during bleak times for he was there as indeed I was on the very first day of change from farmhouse to inn.

George was a gentleman farmer, retired. Harris Tweed jacket, yellow 'weskit' with leather buttons, the bottom button always open as is the way, and with a gold chain showing where a Hunter watch rested in one pocket. Moleskin trousers and heavy brogues, which shone like glass made up the rest. A true countryman was George. He'd done everything from hunting, shooting, fishing and farming and if you didn't like it he'd nod and accept you for what you believed in as long as you didn't tell him you were right and he was wrong sort of thing. I got on well with him and was justly pleased for nature conservationists were a newish breed and some country folk looked at me as if I was from another planet. When I first told him what I did he said at least I didn't wear a blanket and sandals, an awkward image conservationists had gotten from somewhere or other.

One night when I was early down the road and had been picked up and taken to the door by Brian in his car I sat in George's place without thinking as Brian handed me a Mackeson. As I took my first sip in George walked and I still recall the look of shock and disbelief in his eyes as he saw me sipping my drink, on 'his' bar stool of all places.

"Usual George." Brian said as George nodded with his eyes fixed on me. Coins hit the bar top rather hard and Brian was grinning as he placed George's Grouse before him.

"Evening George", I nodded and smiled.

"Aye", he said and turning about he stared pointedly at all the other empty seats in the bar.

"Rainy old day George" I said in the time honoured way of beginning a conversation with the weather.

"Oh, you notice some things then," Was his stiff reply.

The Grouse and water disappeared to be replaced by another, the landlord knowing well the habits of the old man.

Hazel appeared and seeing George standing by the bar stared at me with an amazed look, forgot to say 'hello', and promptly left again.

Truth to tell I had not thought one bit about that particular seat as I entered the inn with Brian from the cold and rain. Furthest from the old blackened oak door seemed warmest and so I had chosen.

As the light dawned I grinned. Old George stared. I could see him thinking only idiots grin for no good reason and he inwardly satisfied himself I must be an idiot to both sit on his stool and grin at nothing. I caught Brian's eye. He was doing his best to stop smiling.

"Is it still raining Brian?" I asked quietly.

"Dunno Tree, probably is", he said with his eyes twinkling.

I strolled to the window peering out into the murk. "Yep, still pouring down." I remarked turning again from the window.

Old George was in 'his' seat, Grouse in one gnarled fist, pipe in the other, his lined face in repose. All the world was put to rights.

Some years later when the inn changed hands and improvements were made to provide more room Old George fell of his stool seven nights in a row before he schooled himself to the fact that the pillar he had rested on for years had been removed to enlarge the room.

19

Winter Goes On and On and...

"I'm fed up".

The loud cheerless voice was attention seeking. I was chatting to Henry just inside the inn door and we looked to see Nick, a carpenter on the nearby estate talking over-loud to June the barmaid, a sure sign he'd had at least his second half of best bitter.

"Much more frozen food out of packets and I swear Jane will have frostbitten fingers preparing it" he moaned loudly.

The bar went quiet. There were half a dozen of us in, the others really local.

"Never mind dear," June smiled warmly at Nick. "Perhaps Jane has so much else to do she hasn't the time you have to spare in here".

Nick look startled and someone chuckled.

"Mind you" he said. "She's a great cook, a great cook and maybe I'll take a bottle of Leib' back with me to have with our meal. I'd best be moving on" He paid for the bottle of white wine and left hurriedly.

June looked at Henry and me and winked.

"A wise old head on young shoulders there Tree, and a lovely one." Henry said and I nodded.

"Yes Henry. Takes a special sort of strength to do that job. I couldn't do it".

"I suppose so. Reminds me of some years ago of a similar young waitress in a restaurant. I ordered tomato soup to begin my meal and was brought vegetable soup. I told her of the error and the poor girl looked flustered, then she brightened and said, 'I know what' as she smiled at me. Do you know, she crossed tomato out from the order pad, wrote in vegetable and went off with the most delightful smile. I drank every drop". He sighed.

Jack Piper came into the bar shaking raindrops from his waterproof.

"Don't say it's raining again Jack" I groaned, for it had been one of the wettest winters on record and the countryside was a sponge.

"Alright, I won't say it," Jack laughed and took the shandy handed to him by June who knew her locals tipple.

"How goes it Jack?" Henry asked the sinewy countryman who travelled the area gardening for all and sundry.

"Oh I'm in the doghouse again. I'm in it so often I could win prizes at Crufts, Henry"

We knew the full story was about to flow as Jack took long swigs of his drink and leaned over the bar. "Twas like this. We went down by the river this morning for a stroll cos the rain has put me off a lot of the work I'd normally be doing. We leaned on the bridge watching for trout to move up and I said to my missus, look how happy them trout be darting about. She said how did I know they were happy or not. It lasted two hours arguing that out, all the way home and right through dinner time. Coo, she didn't see I was teasing and she was in a right old tizz."

I tried to imagine two hours arguing whether fish were happy or not and gave up.

"It was a pleasant morning for a walk though Jack" Henry said, "until the rain came in later that is".

"Perfect. I wished I wasn't off work really but I couldn't go grass cutting, too wet."

"Why do you wish you weren't off work if it was perfect Jack? Henry asked.

"Well, such a lovely morning, if I'd been working I would have had the time off to enjoy it".

Jack downed the remainder of his shandy and shouting cheerio to everyone strode out of the inn to go back to his beloved wife.

Jake Skinner was suddenly beside us and I nodded to June to include him in my buying the next round.

"Thanks Tree. Grandson has been over to see us today. Daughter brought him over as school is on half term. He said the Headmaster died two weeks ago but it was alright as they'd found a new one, and Gipsy their spaniel is pregnant." Jake smiled and drank from his glass, then he continued. "I asked him whether he'd noticed how the dog was getting bigger with the pups growing inside her. He said no, but he'd noticed her head getting smaller and smaller."

"Lovely" I murmured.

"Aye. He's a good lad. Sharp for an eight year old. Daughter wants to start him at Sunday School but he isn't too keen. Missus tried to gently persuade him. She said he'd learn all about Heaven. Tommy looked up at her and said he would rather it was a surprise".

We laughed. Henry asked after Jake's wife.

"Oh, touch of the rheumatics but alright otherwise. Funny thing last Sunday though. We'd gone for our regular stroll down to the shop for the paper and a chat with anybody on the way. This car pulled up and the driver asked the way to Lynton. I told him the road to follow and he said how quiet 'twas in these parts. Well missus said just wait 'til the church comes out then all hell will break loose. Cor, was her face red I can tell ee."

We drank up. It was just on nine O'clock and we decided to move on. Outside as we were bidding each other farewell a youngish couple came down the road to enter the inn, calling out to Jake and nodding cheerily to Henry and I.

Jake looked after them. "New to the village they are. From Exeter, nice couple but he is a real townie. The woman, Jackie was telling my missus she had a vase of pussy willow on their TV back along for two weeks. Then she changed it for Forsythia when that came into flower. When her husband came home from work he sat watching the box after dinner and suddenly shouted out excitedly that the pussy willow had come into bloom at last."

We parted, enjoying the humour that is the best and loveliest part of people.

20

Smithie & Co

It was pouring with rain. In fact it seemed as if had been pouring with rain forever. I had become used to it and a sunny day would be almost a shock to the system. Had I not been monitoring a waterway for signs of otters I would not have been in the vicinity of the trusty inn on this particular bleak day but as it was wet and cold, and I was wet and cold, the log fire and a hot pasty were too much to resist.

"Awful day Tree baint it". Old Smithies voice sounded from behind the door in the big pew seat where he was wont to sit whenever he was in.

"The day's alright Smithie, but the weather isn't so good" I greeted him.

"Aye, you're right there, though I suppose the rain is alright too and we always need water. Give us three days in July without it and everyone's crying out for the stuff". Smithie puffed at his old briar pipe. I observed him through a fuzzy halo of blue smoke, some sort of black shag he smoked from his Navy days. A mans tobacco, he reckoned. He grinned when I waved the smoke away.

"Never seen you smoke have I?" he asked.

"No and you never will. Can't stand the stuff myself".

He chuckled. I'll have to keep it away from you then. I began when I was young to impress the girls. All the big film stars smoked in they days. We tried to imitate them, be like them, used to work sometimes too", he laughed.

"Image eh Smithie". I replied. I tried to imagine which film stars. Smithie was tiny, a jockeyish type and more like a ferret at first sight, and second sight too come to that. Ferret Wayne? Ferret Mitchum. It didn't ring true somehow. He was more John Mills size really. I asked him who he used to imitate to impress the girls.

"Well now. Twas Lauren Bacall I liked. Still see her on the telly with Bogart. Now she knew how to hold a cigarette.

I was glad Henry walked in at that moment.

"Hello Tree, hello Smithie Smith. Looks like rain, " was his greeting as he doffed his wide brimmed hat and sprayed us both.

"Feels like rain too" I muttered, wiping my spectacles clear yet again.

Henry chuckled and turned to the bar. "Ah, Inn- keeperess, a half of your amber liquid and one for your goodself, and I'll have one of those things Tree is eating, smells wonderful. Same again for you chaps?" He called.

"Same again," we chorussed.

Henry returned with drinks and pies for all. Smithie looked surprised but pleasantly so and soon swapped pipe for pie.

Henry looked at me and winked. He didn't smoke either. A good tactical move.

"Had to make my hegira from home," he said,. It's been one of those days."

"Good grief Henry. Stay with the English language do" I exclaimed.

"Hegira. A flight to a more desirable place, that is, here" he responded, "Arabic I think".

"Bad day then Henry". It was a statement.

"Just me really Tree. Couldn't write a darned thing and the phone rang every minute. Brought me a headache. I felt filled with asperity. It'll soon go now though fellows". He sat back and bit into his pie.

"Asperity" said Smithie. "Ah, they'm those new dissolving asprin things I keep hearing about. Yes, your headache should soon go now Henry".

I too bit into my pie as Henry sighed.

21

Rainy Night with George-ia

Heavy rain beat against the inn walls, blown by the gale force winds gusting across the landscape. The sign proclaiming the inn's name squeaked on its hinges as it swung eerily to and fro, the country road awash with water reflecting the light from windows and the wrought iron lantern outside. At any moment one might expect a stagecoach to round the corner to allow its passengers to quaff ale by the cheery fire within. I stood beneath the small porch watching the shadow of the sign swing back and forth upon the roadway's glistening surface for we were a mite early for opening time.

"A foul night" Henry muttered in understatement huddling back into the old inn's doorway.

Old George joined us. It took a moment or two to see who it was for he was sensibly clad in sou'wester hat and shining black waterproof reaching to his feet.

"Got to have the right gear you know!" he yelled directly into my ear, rendering me half deaf. I had these oilskins when I was in the Army and Navy you know. I come here to get wet inside, not outside".

"What. You were in both services?" George was full of surprises.

He looked at me wonderingly. "No, the Army and Navy Stores, the shop that used to be by the bus station in town."

I knew where he meant though the shop had been gone for nigh on ten years.

"I liked the old days best," he shouted again to make himself heard above the wind though I think the sou'wester over his ears was the cause of the trouble. I asked him why.

"Cos I was younger then of course," he laughed. "Here, let me get in nearer the door" he said squeezing Henry and I towards the road. Just then without warning the inn door opened. Outwards.

George did a half dance, a sort of teetering fox-trot and promptly sat in the road as Brian poked his head out and shouted that the pub was open.

We hoisted George upright and he was first to the bar to order. Brian grinned at him and said he should not come to the inn drunk. The log fire blazed in the hearth and we were soon served with our favourite hot pasties and a drink as George stood by the fire to dry his trousers, keeping his eye on 'his' seat all the while. Brian was still grinning an ill concealed grin as George glared and steamed.

"How's the garden then George?" He asked smilingly.

"Garden!" George's voice rose an octave higher than usual. It's rained solid for days, why ask about the garden?"

"Well I saw your beans still up and about when I was passing the other day". Brian answered him.

"Ah well I've left them for the time being. So much rain the bean sticks took leaf. Never known that before."

Brian stared. "What? Burst into leaf, your bean sticks?"

"Aye, every single one" There was a gleam in George's eye.

"I must come and photograph that tomorrow George". Brian was a keen amateur photographer always about the area with his camera. He went off to tell his wife.

George grinned. "I want some photos of my daughter and she'll be out with us tomorrow. Just right that". He was a cunning old fox but from where I stood I could see Brian hovering with a crate of bottles and then he moved away.

A moment or two later the door latch moved noisily up and down. We all turned to see who was entering the inn. A strange crouching figure could be seen in the darkness wearing what looked all the world like a top hat. Behind the figure hail pounded the roadway and then the door slammed shut with a crash, the figure remaining outside.

I went to the door and opened it. There was no one to be seen, nor in the roadway beyond.

"Well I'll be jiggered," said George, "What was that?"

"Ghost perhaps". Brian was back at the bar. "The inn is haunted you know".

"Haunted?! I've lived in the parish all my life and the only ghost is the one up by the church seen on All Hallows Eve". George knew his local history.

Brian stared at him, his face serious.

"It's kept quiet. Don't want to lose trade. Anyway the ghost haunted the farm originally, before it was an inn. It's only been seen again since I did that renovation work. I was told about him when we moved here. Sir Hector somebody or other I think".

George stared at Brian aghast. "Sir Hector? That's Sir Hector Knighton. That's him up in the churchyard. Before even the manor days. What's he doing down here?"

Brian's face was a picture of concentrated seriousness as he stared hard at George.

"He comes here once a year. Latches on to a local and follows him home. It's only once a year, so not worth talking about. Usually he comes after closing time so I never say anything.

"A local you say, he follows a local?" He eyed the two of us worriedly.

"Yes a villager. Not like these two". Brian nodded at us.

George stared uneasily. "Bloomin rain. Should be more people in," he said.

Brian grinned. "Not a chance. Not in this weather George".

Then the sound of the door rattling came again but no one entered. Henry went to the door, then to the window, saying there was not a soul about.

George rose from his seat and went to the window, peering into the gloom intently. He turned to Brian. "Perhaps I'll borrow a torch from you Brian, seeing it's darker than usual tonight."

Brian agreed affably and George, visibly happier returned to his seat.

"We'll take you home in the car George" Henry said. "We can rejoin our road from the crossroads with no problem".

"Now that'd be kind. Only cos of the weather mind. This ghost stuff don't bother me none". He settled back sipping his Grouse and watching the door.

Brian leaned towards Henry and me at the bar. "I have an old top hat upstairs" he grinned.

"Yes I sort of thought you might have" I said. "A titfer-tat for the photos eh?"

"Very droll Tree" chuckled Henry, "country life is exciting".

22

More Wintry Tales

Henry and I were sitting in the pew seat just inside and behind the door when it banged open and in came the wind, a pile of leaves in reds and golds and a young man of around 25 or so.

"Pint of the best" he muttered to Brian.

"The best what" growled mine host who quite rightly liked a 'please' at the end of a request.

"Oh, the brown ale there" the fellow answered still in some land of dreams and private thoughts.

I sat back against the high backed seat enjoying the peace and warmth for we had walked some six miles along lanes and the narrow road because it was a Saturday and walking is a good thing to be doing at weekends.

"The fellow is unhappy Tree" Henry observed.

"Agree with you Henry, he comports himself in sad manner methinks," I agreed as I also saw how he slumped somewhat dejectedly over the bar.

"Now, now Tree", Henry's tone was reproving. "I can tell by your tone you are in your non-involvement mood".

I nodded in tacit agreement. I knew Henry was not so much upbraiding me as remarking on my reluctance to become involved with the problems of strangers, a reluctance I bore quite happily as being 'my nature' just as I hated gossipy people who live in 'the space' of others. Actually Henry was just the same. He also hated gossip but because of his standing in his profession he was more social than I and had a better aptitude for sociability.

The young man suddenly turned, seeing us for the first time since he had entered the inn, no doubt having heard our voices though not the content.

"May I join you?" He enquired.

"Yes", said Henry, "or no if my friend here does not agree".

I waved my hand to an empty seat opposite us the onus firmly placed upon me to make the welcoming gesture. The fellow came over and sat down, emptying his glass and staring into it. He looked dulled, deflated, almost lifeless and I felt uneasy yet concerned.

"I'll get the drinks in" I said and went to the bar.

We were the only three in as yet, the usual week night 'rush' of two or three people. Even George was not in his usual seat. I took the drinks back and we all sipped half-heartedly.

"My dog has just died, " the man said.

"I'm sorry." We both said it at the same time. Henry and I were both dog lovers and knew well the 'holes' left in a body when a faithful friend passes on. "How long was your dog with you?" I continued.

"Fourteen years. I know he was a good age but it doesn't help".

"No, it bloody well doesn't" Henry said. "A dog is a dog and that's a great deal".

" If you gave him a happy life then know it and know the dog knew it too. Wherever he is now he'll know that". I said.

Henry stared hard at the floor and I knew he was remembering an animal friend he had lost in tragic circumstances. It seemed best to say as little as possible.

"Nature calls." I rose to walk through the bar giving Brian a nod as I did so. He followed me to the pool room where I explained the situation, Brian's face assuming an expression of deep understanding. Ones animal friends elicit a universal response from others when they are ill or have passed on.

"Oddly enough I may have got just the answer, but go back and expect sharp tactics". Brian said. "Go back and keep him chatting and I wont be long". Within a minute Hazel had taken over the bar and I heard Brian's car driving away from outside.

I wandered back to the table. Henry and the sad man were in conversation. Henry had a way of getting people to open up under the most difficult circumstances. Real psychologists are born not trained. They were talking about cars, my most unfavourite subject along with football and soaps so I sat back and let them chatter away. Two customers entered the bar and then I heard a car halt outside and shortly after Brian was serving drinks. He caught my eye and nodded in a way that meant all is well.

Two or three minutes later Jed Hargreaves entered the bar and nodded to us. I hadn't seen him at the inn for months for he tended to stay around the Manor farmstead and rarely ventured forth.

"Evening all. How's everything then Henry", Jed asked, standing squarely in front of us with a very obvious sheepdog pup held to his chest.

"What's this then Jed? Baby sitting for Jess?" I asked, knowing Jed's bitch collie well from my wanderings in the valley where Jed had some fine sheep.

"Aye. Got one here that I can't keep on the farm and worse still the fellow who was supposed to take her says he can't. House trained, the lot, but I've got three dogs as tis". He rubbed the dog's ears gently and went to the bar where Brian handed him a drink.

"What is she called?" the sad man called after him, rising to follow Jed to the bar.

"Bramble," Jed said. Don't suppose you want a dog do you?" Jed looked the fellow straight in the eyes.

"Bramble," the man smiled as the dog pricked up her ears at the sound of her name.

"A good name don't you think Tree?" Jed called to me.

"None better, and no better breed than collies or collie crosses in my book" I answered.

Henry looked at me. "The next dog I get I'll call Tree after you".

"I'll drink to that Henry" I grinned.

The sad man was rubbing the collie pups head. "I'll have her", he said. "My wife will be over the moon, what'll you take for him". The fellow had straightened and become alive.

Jed stared at him and at the collie. "I'll take your word he'll always have a good home young feller, you hear me good".

There was a twitch in Jed's chin for he loved all animals.

The no longer sad man took the dog gently, holding him lovingly.

"Here, I'll give you our address. Call and see her and us anytime you are over our way. She's beautiful. I'll take her home straight away.

Jed went to the bar as the man left with his new friend. Brian poured him a whisky and winked across at Henry and me.

23

Pool Night

H enry was far from being a real local though he had
lived in North Devon longer than I, by reason of his
age difference. I was a born Devonian but other than
this difference we were very alike and I tended to relate better
to older people better than young as it was.

Henry drank beer. He drank beer moderately and slowly,
enjoying it for what it was and the inn for what it was.

"I come here simply because I like the place, there's no
other reason to do so is there?" He would comment with his
statements having a hint of a query in them yet firm, Henry
believing in what he said and saying what he believed. Henry
was a wise man and an observer par excellence.

It was Pool Night. Pool Night is important, like darts or skit-
tles night though there was no skittle alley at the inn. Pool is a
fine game, it is fun and thought provoking, serious to the pool
teams of course, but to me just for the fun of it like all games.
Competitiveness has its good points but on Pool Night the
corner around the pool area became electric, amusingly so at
times for I have seen people walk away to the other side of the
bar just to cough rather than be the reason for a missed shot.

Henry and I were seated near the inn door deep in conversation. We had been relegated there by the shocked stares of a
tense crowd of locals who had gathered to observe 'their' team
battle against the rivals who were currently top of the league.
Henry had committed an act of gross indecency. He had called
'well played' aloud when one of the opposing team had made
a particularly fine shot to win on the black ball. Now the teams
were equal with all to play for and Henry would be remembered for the rest of that evening as having rooted for the
other side.

"Steve is playing now". We heard the comment from someone at the bar, an earnest looking young man we recognised as one of the players. He stood on tiptoe hardly daring to look, biting the nails of one hand nervously as he watched. "He's getting over the 'flu' and may not be on form" he added. It was like listening to David Coleman explaining why one of our athletes had lost at the Olympics.

Pool balls clicked sharply in the distance and there was a murmur as a ball could be heard to rumble along its carefully engineered tramway in the dark interior of the pool table. Again the click of ivory, or whatever passes for ivory these days in this more enlightened age, and again the rumble of a pocketed ball.

The earnest young man looked pleased and stopped biting his nails. He stood on tiptoe again, hitting his head on a low beam, forgetting he had moved forward a pace or two. He glared up at the beam, smoothing his hair back into place the game momentarily forgotten. This was high drama. Henry and I laughed. Two girls were giggling loudly. Girl friends of two of the players they had to stand by in support of their men. One a tall leggy girl holding a tall glass lost control and giggled helplessly. Those close by turned to her reprovingly, which served to make matters worse. She took a swig of her drink, obviously hoping it would help. Henry doubled up as she choked with laughing, spraying the young man who had hit his head on the beam.

This was now sheer beauty. Head -dapper moved in panic to one side, bumping his neighbour, which began a row of dominoes effect on the crowd watching the game. There was a loud "'Oi!' Watch it then," from the pool table area and a cry of "shame, shame".

"How is it going June?" Henry asked the barmaid.

"Well, Steve was doing very well but someone moved forward and jostled his cue as he was about to play a shot and he potted the opponents ball by mistake, Tisn't very sweet out there".

"He lost then, did Steve?" Said Henry.

"Oh Yes, all over now barring the inquest" she replied.

At the edge of the crowd the young fellow who had been sprayed was getting dirty looks but he was intent on passing on the glare to the leggy girl who turned to grin at Henry.

"Of course Henry, you started all this you know" I chuckled.

"Perish the thought Tree. But it does show how a simple chain effect can play havoc. Everything we do has its effect on everything else. We must experiment again on the next Pool Night".

"Perish the thought Henry" I said, "Perish the thought".

24

Owl Evening

David Millard and his wife entered the bar, stared about and made a beeline for where I was sitting. "Glad you are here Tree, there's something odd out there in the road".

This was from Sarah, David's lovely young wife.

Several raucous guffaws sounded about. "Horse went by just now missus!" Someone called as Sarah Millard turned a deep pink.

"No you silly man." Sarah looked around for the joker. "It knocked my hat off".

Even more laughter. "Must have been Pegasus missus" called some classically well read wag.

David was trying to keep a straight face. "No. Truly Tree. As we came across the car park there was a thud and Sarah's hat literally flew off. Here look at it, covered in mud". He handed me a wide brimmed Barbour hat, which was indeed wet and muddy from a skirmish with the ground outside.

"Tawny owl I reckon. I saw one flying about recently in the field beside the car park, and seeing it's dark out there, well lets take a look while Sarah buys the drinks."

Sarah smiled and went to the bar where her hat was passed around for all to see.

"Yes Definitely horse," someone said.

"Got good taste too, knocking it off." Said another.

We could hear Sarah jovially telling them what a frightful lot they were as we went out into the darkness.

I told David it was not uncommon for owls to defend territory or late young and even as we chatted there came the sharp 'kee-wick' of a hunting owl and we saw the silent shape glide by us along the top of the hedgerow just six feet from where we stood.

"Wonderful sight" David said, "But I'll shift the car down nearer the inn lights I think".

"Probably a good idea" I replied as we watched the owl glide down and then up to perch on the top of the inn sign watching us. With the vehicle safely parked in the brighter lit area of the car park we went back inside. Sarah had drinks ready at a small table near the fire. She was smiling broadly.

"Where's your hat dear?" David enquired as he told her of the owl sighting.

Sarah pointed. Roger, one of the locals was smugly sitting on a barstool with the hat set rakishly and far too small on his head.

We chatted about owls and such for a while, enjoying the log fire and cosy surroundings. Minutes later 'Chippy' Kerslake came into the bar holding his tweed trilby which was wet and muddy, a mystified look on his face.

"Tawny Owl!" came a great chorus of voices as he stood staring in bewilderment at us all.

"Blimey" Chippy said, "Felt more like a horse".

25

The Fireside Chat Club

J arvis and Fred were crouched over the log fire reminiscing when I wandered into the bar. "May I join you chaps"
I asked.
'What are we drinking did you say Tree? Ours is pints
please, good of you to ask". Jarvis looked up with a smile.

It was heading towards the end of the year and I'd been
working at the Sanctuary cleaning out nestboxes rather later in
the year than usual, and removing fallen branches from the
paths following the recent gales and rains. I crossed to the bar
where a grinning Brian had two pints already poured along
with a Mackeson, my own favourite thirst quencher.

As usual in midweek the bar was quiet. George was in his
usual seat 'Grousing' and reading a newspaper and Hazel was
deep in her crossword. Both looked up and asked how I was
and off I strolled to the fireplace seats with the drinks. I sat and
gazed around at the warm painted room, the polished horse
brasses and woodwork reflecting the dancing firelight and
sipped my beverage appreciatively.

Jarvis was also called Fred but as he was always about with
Fred, who was called Pinn, everyone locally called Jarvis by his
surname, Fred Pinn being several years ahead of Jarvis in the
lifespan of things.

"Ah, thanks lad, Kind of ee to ask, sittee down there where
you'm sat" Jarvis said as Fred nodded his thanks.

"We were talking about working in the countryside. I've
worked all my life but somehow it seems longer than that,"
Fred said. Course, I'm 67 now so I spends my time in the
garden, save when I do the churchyard grass and hedges".

"Been doing that a while now haven't you" Jarvis said,
drawing Fred on to chatter the more as he finished his first
pint in order to get to the one I'd brought them.

Fred nodded. "Aye, 30 years. Ever since old Bill Lang had to give it up. Well ee fell down daid in a grave ee was digging so ee could hardly have carried on with the job. Anyway 'tis a closed churchyard now like so many of em but I hope they don't put the gravestones all round the sides like some churches do. Don't seem right do it".

Jarvis shook his head in firm agreement. I glanced at the two old timers, brought up with the village life and rural ways, not happy with cost-cutting modernity and the disappearing way of life gradually being eroded by some in-comers.

Fred went on. "Funny old place though at times. Peaceful mostly but it gets its moments. I was cutting grass last summer and old Mary from the village was putting flowers on her husband. Her didn't see me squatting behind old Bill Lewis's headstone, 1895 ee died, and I heard her say Jimmie you be better off there, the bloomin rent's gwane up again next week".

There was a touch of pathos in the remark. I felt suddenly blessed that I was relatively young and fit. Old Mary I knew was well past 80 and probably waiting to join her husband.

Fred continued, "And Harold from the old mill cottages, ee without much schooling. Ee come up to me the other morning and said could ee look round at the flowers as we did a better show in our churchyard than where ee lives. Ee spent nigh on two hours walking around looking at the chrysanths and all.

"Times is different now Fred" Jarvis said. "All this cremating and chucking your ashes about. Cor you could end up in the sink on somebody else's spuds couldn't ee Tree". He chuckled deeply into his glass of ale.

Jarvis drank deeply and went on refreshed. " I remember when I was a lad working on Mays Farm. John May said I was to dig a ditch along the edge of the vegetable gardens to help drain them. Ee gives me a Devon shovel, you don't see them used much now, and off I went. Course I was only 14 so I looked for the softest soil and got to digging. I worked along the edge of the huge vegetable gardens all day. Well about four in the afternoon up comes John May. Course we called him maister in those days. Ee was ranting and raving. You daft beggar Jarvis, ee shouted, what's the good of a ditch up at the top of the slope, a drainage ditch goes down the bottom. Ee was jumping about fit to burst and I stepped back a pace a bit scared like and fell right in to the ditch I'd dug. Maister started shouting again. What did I tell you! If you'd dug it in the proper place you wouldn't have fallen in!"

"Course, next day I had to dig another ditch down the bottom. Then ee got me to fill in the top ditch with manure and I grew the longest and most productive row of broad beans and runner beans the parish has ever seen. Cor did my back ache but 'twas a good job and we got on well Jack and me over the years rest his soul".

It was lovely listening to the two of them. The old farm days when everyone mucked in at harvest time are long gone and sadly missed I'm sure. Bread, cheese and cider in clome jars. I still have some of those jars today. Would that such times came back.

We have had the best of the countryside and possibly its characters for they were as close to nature as men and women get.

"Aye" Fred said. "John May was a fine man and a good farmer. A huge man always with a coloured neckerchief as I remember him. I scrumped his apples one year and had my shirt filled up with them. He suddenly appeared from nowhere and chased me summat terrible across three fields and down Church Lane. I only got away cos ee couldn't get through the hedge where I did.

"Two days later ee put his hand on my shoulder in the village shop. I nigh on wet meself. Ee said in my ear you might be a good runner Freddie Pinn but I gave you a rough time staying in front didn't I?"

Fred grinned at the memory. "Then ee kicked my backside out of the shop and I took to scrumping apples somewhere else after that".

The scrumping of apples was a country schoolboy tradition along with playing conkers. If you were caught scrumping a clip around the ear was an end to it, the catcher almost certainly recalling his own scrumping days. If you told your parents you had had a clip around the ear for scrumping, you got another clip. It was the way of it, the best way, and taught you to respect your elders as teaching you rights and wrongs.

We chatted on. I recalled my own boyhood in the 40s, the War ending when I was eight. There were local and village policemen then, often patrolling on bicycles. There was little or no vandalism then. Ringing doorbells and scrumping, they were the great adventures of childhood and discipline was far better.

I remember a PC Brownscombe grabbing me one summer's night as I was running home late from playing in the fields. "Did you knock on Bessie Milton's door and make her come all downstairs?" he asked me. I told him I hadn't. It actually wasn't me for I got on well with Bessie and used to fetch her shopping after school.

"Well that's just in case you do then" he said and clipped my ear. A protege of Judge Jefferies probably.

"But they dealt with us fair and square as a rule" Fred said." I remember climbing onto my bike to get over a wall to scrump apples one day. I was just climbing out over again when I saw the village Bobby a ways along the road. Of course I leapt on my bike to race off down the road when it fell to bits underneath me and I sat there listening to the policeman laughing his head off as he walked on up the hill. Crafty old beggar".

"Last orders please!" Brian was shouting. Time had passed all too quickly, but pleasantly.

And there would be other times.

26

Rebirth

Winter had passed by in its usual rather slow fashion with March being one of those 'in like a lion out like a lamb' affairs that led into a gentle beginning for April. It was a joy to see the days lengthening again with primroses and violets following the   masses of celandines everywhere. Already the first chiff chaff calls have been heard throughout the Westcountry and those of us whose ears were tuned to bird calls were poised for the first liquid songs of willow warblers.

The inn's log fire still welcomes the weary traveller, the hostelry very busy now from Friday nights and over the weekends, quieter during the weeknights which is when I tended to visit if at all, following work at the Sanctuary. It was on such a day when I had been helping with a tree that had fallen in gales, from the Sanctuary and out into the neighbouring farmers field that I felt a Mackeson tonic and hot pie would boost the spirit.

I had agreed with the farmer that he would chain saw the tree into logs, which would remove the obstruction and he would keep the logs for his fire, a sensible country style working arrangement, which sorted out the problem.

Thus it was that I found myself once more amongst old friends who tolerated my comings and goings as 'the bird man' on an evening when three of the locals had come together in one vehicle for a chat and drop of liquid refreshment, and Jack Snell with his dog.

"Tis a harder life for kids today".

Joe McBride leaned back against the fireside wall, which always became warmed when the log fire was blazing. He stretched his old legs out contentedly, looking around at the four of us on the plank seat opposite. Bruce the retired water bailiff, John Bamford a retired schoolteacher who always celebrated his birthday at the inn, Jack Snell who always brought his docile sheepdog Ben with him, and Cyril who still worked as a farm labourer on the estate across the hill.

John, who was always willing to wax eloquent on education yesterday and today rose to the bait. "Why's it harder for the kids of today then Joe?" he asked.

"Well when we were kids we'd walk to school and back every day and we'd run to keep warm in winter. Now they all stands up by the church shivering and freezing until the school bus gets here. Tis harder today".

No one bothered to argue.

"Still cold though at nights" said Cyril. Brass monkey weather as they calls it."

Cyril was another of the parish bike riders. A heavy black Raleigh with 28ins wheels he was always ready to show anyone. He'd had it forever and yet the left hand side of the road always eluded him. Cyril always appeared over the brows of hills aiming straight down the middle and he'd never had an accident in all his years. Everybody got out of Cyril's way. I'd seen vehicles stop and pull in to the hedgebanks rather than try to pass him going the other way.

"I haven't seen any brass monkeys about have you Tree?" Joe asked staring across at me as the wildlife person in the group.

"Well you wont will you" Cyril replied. "They'm screwed to the decks of ships. They was what the cannon balls rested on beside the guns." He went into depth about the derivation of the term.

"Coo, fancy that and all these years I've thought the monkey's balls"...

"Enough!" Hazel the landlady's voice came loud across the room and Joe shut up.

John Bamford took his pipe from his mouth and put it in his pocket, an act that always alarmed me but his dark suits always seemed smart and without signs of bonfires.

"There would be many more good parents about if their time was not taken up bringing up their children".

We all stared at him. He was somewhere about a subject behind which was a peculiar way he had of joining a conversation. A disjointed joining if there was such a thing.

"That's a profound thought John". I said.

"Well Tree, it is as close to the truth as one gets if one thinks about it".

"Pubs aint for thinking John" said Cyril quickly, anticipating a long speech on education and parenthood in the modern world.

John sighed and gazed into the fire through his pint glass of amber liquid, losing himself in his thoughts once more.

"Tomorrow night" announced Cyril, obviously delighted to have forestalled John's speech, "I'm going to have a big night. I'm going to turn my electric blanket up to medium and get an early night with a Richard Jefferies book".

"Sheer luxury Cyril" I agreed.

"Don't hold with electric blankets. All them live wires about your body. Might wake up daid". Old Joe had spoken his mind and a conversation ensued about the old days of not so long ago when we would get out of bed on freezing mornings hopping about on freezing lino covered floors, holding a shirt in front of the fire to warm it.

It was Joe again with his lovely mix of phrases.

"Mind you," he continued, "missus gave me an electric razor years ago and I likes that. Kicks up such a racket I cant hear her going on in the mornings"

"People don't whistle like they used to". Cyril completely changed the subject.

"They do Cyril." I said. "They still whistle with their mouths".

"No, no. I mean we all used to whistle. Hardly hear anyone whistle these days".

John Bamford awoke from his contemplation of the fire. "You know that's absolutely right. We did whistle a lot years ago. We'd whistle as we marched along the roads when I was in the Army too.

Kids at school rarely whistle a tune. Odd that, a dying art perhaps".

Bruce, who had been quiet throughout the chit chat suddenly spoke up. "When I was water bailiffing and the night was particularly creepy which they sometimes were, I used to whistle to keep myself company. Funny that but it would relieve the tension a bit".

"I think we do that to show nonchalance just in case there is anyone about hidden in the dark". John said thoughtfully.

Cyril chuckled. "I've just been thinking. How could the youngsters of today whistle to the sort of music they listen to. Couldn't be done. Perhaps that's why there's so much vandalism today."

We went quiet, waiting for words of wisdom that would explain the point Cyril was making.

"Well", he said realising we were slightly off his wavelength at least for the moment. "We used to whistle all the old tunes didn't we, happy go lucky like. We never went round writing on people's walls and breaking things. When you have a nice tune in your head you are happy with your lot. You can't do that with today's music you see. Think about it".

John Bamford grinned. "Pubs are not for thinking Cyril".

PART THREE

The Tree of Life
A Look at My Ancestry

Introduction

From ancient Stone Age days when the first words he heard were to leave a lasting impression on his fertile mind Trevor Og Beer became a living legend, or was it a foot? That is, a leg-end.

Will we ever know? Will we ever care?

Those words, uttered by his early ancestors Ogadam and Ogeve were, "Ugh, urff, Mmmm, Ug-og-ig, fetch me a new fig leaf".

It was this search for fig leaves that led Beer into the world of natural history with descendents down through the ages who made their mark at one thing or another, sometimes two things or another and so it was that the Beer legend was born, a name to be found today on many gardens in many pubs, Beer Gardens named specifically after the young boy known as 'half pint' during his schooldays and mitching days alike.

It was during these formative years that Beer was top of the class for absenteeism, especially during summer afternoons, that he really began to learn about the countryside and places where he could hide to watch wildlife and the bicycle roaming Schools Inspector.

1

In His Own Words

Trevor Beer the naturalist of today. I recall well at the age of 6 years that I saw several bats flying about one evening catching grasshoppers and crickets. I immediately identified them as cricket bats. Indeed I was never stumped for an answer and had a wicket sense of humour.

Picking flowers from the local rectory garden at the age of 7 I was caught and thrashed by the vicar who interestingly enough was actually called Parsons. On arrival home I was thrashed again for telling my parents why I had been thrashed by the vicar.

'Picking flowers is not a good idea', I wrote in a school essay next day and so was born my interest in conservation.

My uncanny ability to foresee events added to my reputation when I was seen to stand by the rectory gate the following week as the vicar leapt on his bike which promptly fell to pieces as he cycled off down the steep country road just as I had predicted. Some say the vicar hitting the road so hard with his nose and mouth as he leapt over the handlebars was later copied by several Popes of Rome when they went around the world to visit new countries but no-one is sure if the vicar's comments as he raised himself from the road he had been kissing were actually Latin or some more obscure phrases. Those nearby at the time said he may have been drinking as he referred to 'the devil Beer'a few times.

A strange rapport developed between us, the vicar throwing large stones at me to attract my attention whenever I passed by the rectory garden. In return I would collect hundreds of cabbage white butterfly caterpillars and slugs from nearby fields and allotments, taking them to the vicar's vegetable plot as part of my wildlife relocation studies.

As the years passed the vicar would wave his stick at me, running down the garden and he would weep when I did not stop to talk to him.

"Come back here you little ....." he would scream loudly and then his wife would appear to lead him indoors shaking.

That he singled me out as his favourite was obvious as he would lurk behind trees and in gateways for me but I was very observant and would suddenly rush by. We would play chasing all over the area until he got out of breath and collapsed in a hedge most times.

One day when I was 10 our teacher asked if any of us wanted to join the church choir so I put my name down on the list she was making. She told me next day the vicar said 'only over his dead body', and I realised then that he wanted me to sing at his funeral one day. I called out to him in the street I hoped it would be soon as my parents were thinking of moving home. 'God be praised' he shouted and we had one last game of chasing up and down the street but he never caught me and one day we were told he had moved to another more peaceful area in the heart of London.

I missed him for all of two hours then went on with my wildlife studies, exploring the countryside and becoming very fit for I was always out and about. I used to bring things home but my parents never shared my interests and hated finding grass snakes and such about the house. I kept a secret collection of rocks under my brother's beds to try to get them interested but they were peeved when they all got into trouble for the mess and I didn't.

One day after I'd gotten into trouble again for taking home a snake to look after I was told I could not go out for a week as punishment. One evening, in order to study reptile movement patterns, I tied a broken bicycle inner tube to a long length of thread and put it in our communal wash-house in the back yard. I then opened our kitchen window, slowly pulling the thread just as one of our neighbours went along to the outside lavatory.

There was lots of screaming and her husband rushed out and spent ages hitting it with a coal shovel as I pulled it in little jerks across the yard. My father rushed out with a torch and began hitting it, then saw what it was. He said he would give me a good hiding and came in shouting and laughing at the same time, making slapping noises with his hands as he listened to our neighbours calling me names out loud as the woman was crying and whimpering a lot.

I couldn't see why anyone would hit a length of rubber like that or go around crying about it. My father said I could go out evenings after all as it was safer when I wasn't home.

One day we had a talk at school given by a policeman, about security and things and he said he always tied his bike up when he had to leave it anywhere. That night I tied up my neighbour's black Raleigh back wheel to the railings as a favour so he wouldn't get it pinched. He was an Air Raid Warden at the time and he went out and jumped on his bike to ride off and there was this great crash and lots of shouting. I went out and said the policeman had told us all to do it at school and he said just wait until he saw the policeman and words like that and how glad he was I was leaving soon to live somewhere else which I thought was nice of him. He said I caused more injuries than half the German army and they should send me out to the front. I said we were out the front already and he made lots of little squeaking noises like the bats flying overhead.

I was actually quite good at school lessons, especially Reading, English, Art and Science things, but hopeless at Arithmatic. One day, after I had been told off by the teacher for getting all the sums wrong she made me come down from the back row of class to sit in the front as she thought I was fooling about when I wasn't. I suddenly saw all the sums on the black board had adding up signs beside them and I had done all subtractions. I told the teacher who had a look and found I had got them all right if they had been 'take aways'. She took me to the back of the class and asked what I could see and sure enough the signs had all changed!

"You need glasses Beer", she told me and sure enough when we were tested for eyesight one day I had to get glasses to wear. I was not getting all my sums wrong, I could not see the signs properly.

Straight away on wearing glasses I went from 'Half Pint' at school to 'Four Eyes' with those awful little wire frames that are now so popular with spectacle wearers. I hated it and blamed maths so refused to have anything to do with the subject. I got very bad at it and still am to this day, forms and things filling me with dread. But I continued on with the subjects I loved and was always top at those.

We did move home, to my grandparents place as my gran was ill and needed looking after. I remained at my old school on the other side of town and had to walk to and fro, even at lunch times as there were no school dinners and was often soaked to the skin four times a day.

I missed my old haunts in the evenings as it was such a long way to go but I went back every weekend and during the holidays, helping at one or two farms as well as playing in the fields and woods around and about. Great days all, if not as exciting as those of my ancestors, some of whom I will tell you about in the next chapters.

2

Beer the Fisherman

It was thanks to Izaak Beer the greatest angler in all England that Izaak Newton became the Compleat Angler in his day. Beer found Newton sitting on a riverbank one afternoon with a stick and some string. Newton would rest the string on the end of the stick then flick it out over the water, each time losing the string.

"Why don't you tie it on to the end like this", said Beer, showing him how.

"Goodness", cried Newton holding the string and throwing the stick out over the water where it hit a leaping trout. "And it works first time. Now I am compleat!"

"You ought to write a book about that", Beer said as he went on his merry way.

Later that day whilst watching swallows and swifts catching insects Beer thought the flies must be very nutritious. He tied more string onto a stick and began whipping the flies over the water to knock them down to see how they tasted. And so fly fishing was born, Beer later adding tiny hooks to the end of the line as an improvement as after about four years he had not actually caught a fly in this manner but felt it was truly sporting. Then he thought he would make imitation flies in bright colours to tie on the hooks so that the flies zooming about over the water would believe it was a good idea to jump on the hook.

To his sadness he kept catching fish, often large trout and such but never a fly. Beer consoled himself with eating well cooked trout and other fish but eventually gave up fly fishing as futile, his brief excursion into the world of angling soon over. To this very day the sport has never caught on though anglers continue to catch fish in this manner as a tribute to Izaak Beer and his initiative.

3

Iron Age Beer

Even earlier in history than the days of Izaak Beer was Iron Age Beer, the first known blacksmith whose amazing knowledge was hailed by Emperor Haile Delighted of Ethiopia in the days when it was called Esiopia, before map makers spoke with a lisp (lithp).

Haile Delighted said of Beer, "His knowledge of metal is surpassed only by his lack of knowledge.I am proud that he is English and not from my country. There cannot be many books on metal work of this standard about today. Iron Age Beer deserves all he gets for this incredible publication. The book he referred to was short and to the point.

It was Iron Age Beer who invented square chariot wheels to have the tyres already flat in case of punctures. Nero burned Rome down when he heard that Beer was moving there to live.

With nature conservation always in the blood he invented the iron bow and arrow to prevent the felling of yew and willow trees. The weapon could easily be fired by 40 men lifting it together. This was the Golden Age of the hernia, and iron chastity belts, which had to be so carefully fitted. There were 40,000 applicants for the task but unselfish as ever Beer did the job himself. The evil Sheriff of Nottingham, a man called Barren, sorry, Baron Grouch, commissioned a metal shield from Beer who made two types, a circular band of metal with no centre, and an invisible shield which Baron Grouch found very light to handle.

Being no fool Grouch immediately ordered a sword of the same material. This fooled his enemies into thinking he was unarmed so they killed him quite easily.

Beer gave all the invisible money Grouch had paid him with, to the poor and moved to the Westcountry. Old English words

such as 'AAArgh!' and 'B-off!' became household words whenever Beer was about, his contributions to the English native
tongue being considerable. He invented iron goods for everything previously made in wood, his love of trees becoming
known far and wide.

His iron furniture put many furniture removal firms out of
business as people couldn't move house. They could not move
even a chair come to that and having a magnet in ones pocket
could prove fatal.

And then a strange thing happened. Beer became fond of
metal as a material and began using wood to protect metal
resources.

The clanging of church bells changed to a bonking sound,
hence the expression known throughout the land, "who's that
bonking in the belfry, the vicar again?"

Fire engines, helmets and the ends of hosepipes were now
made of wood but when Beer suggested hosing fires with
petrol to save water all the experiments failed and Fire Chiefs
ordered wooden beaters instead. Wooden pokers and toasting
forks did not last long, Beer realising his ideas were too far
ahead of his time, thus he reverted to his skills with metal,
winning the Iron Cross, a medal weighing a ton, which was
pinned on his chest at a special under-sea ceremony by a diver.

Beer, overwhelmed with the honour, could only say "glug-
glug" as he disappeared from view to the sound of cheers from
onlookers.

The Queen, the Prime Minister, The President of the United
States all danced and partied for a week following the medal
ceremony. They issued a statement that Beer was taking an
underwater walking holiday and had gone missing. A 30
second search was made but abandoned due to good weather
and nothing more was heard of Beer for some time.

HOWEVER!!!

As these Beer disappearance decisions had been made by top
level Government brains the medal and anchors, made by
Beer himself had been manufactured in his 'wood' and not his
'Metal' days. Thus it was he floated to the surface and drifted

to Hawaii where he was mistaken for the legendary "He who will rise dripping from the sea on a wooden medallion driven by two anchors" god.

So tough was the treatment Beer received from the beautiful island population of women he decided he would stay only about 90 years while he taught them new ways such as cutting the grass really short for the grass skirts and having 7 days a week holidays and things.

For a long while the Beer saga became quiet as he banned all communications with his now private island where he lived with the totally female population, all males being sent on a self improvement course to rebuild the Lost City of Atlantis on its present site, from maps drawn by Beer himself.

Soon to be published is "Atlantis Mysterious Undersea Walks, The Underwater Ramblers Guide to the Land of No Return".

Stories of his amazing woodworking skills still drifted to the mainland in bottles sent by Beer to keep his English friends happy, or was it miserable. As a professor of Timberology he was lead guitarist with The Carpenters, played with Woody Guthrie and Woody Woodpecker and invented the Vile Inn and other local Pubs. His most famous backing group was Woody Allen, Jimmy Naill, Brad Awl and The Pincer Group.

Using only a saw Beer has made two pieces of wood from one piece. He was a lumberjack in Canada for a while but was fired because he stammered. Apparently shouting, "T-T-T-T-T-T-T-Timber!" was part of the problem. He moved from Lake Eerie, which was named after him, moving to Texas where he became a cattle rustler, unaware that it was against the law. Deported back to England he became a crisp bag rustler in cinemas but, thrown out he decided to take up intricate woodwork and fine art, inventing his own two day course and apprenticeship. He began work on the Monday and was fully qualified by Wednesday, setting about making rude screens for churches. Told later that they should be rood screens he spent the next year carving firewood from bits of stick, which someone was going to throw on a fire, again showing his remarkable abilities as a conservationist.

Rubbing himself all over with grease there was no holding him. Beer fenced off plots of land beside public houses all over Britain, these now being known affectionately as 'Beer Gardens' in his honour.

A letter from the queen saying she wanted to knight him in two weeks was turned down as Beer said he did not want to be a fortnight.

He became well known in high places, Dunkery Beacon, Ben Nevis, even on Everest where he invented double glazing though he was by then so busy he had no windows in his diary.

He was now so well known the rich and famous came to him for work. Beer made a door for Dora Bryan, a bridge for River Phoenix, sent a new bill to Gregory Peck, built the pointy end of a house for Clark Gable, a forestry direction finder for Clint Eastwood, a cheque-book cover for Johnny Cash, and was quite fonda Jane Fonda.

His new villages in America quickly became famous ghost towns and were used in several western films, making him millions of dollars sent to him by ship. Sadly, the year before, Beer had turned his hand to ship building. None of the money reached him. He then simply called the ships permanent submarines and was widely acclaimed for his lateral thinking, and vertical sinking.

Today he passes on his knowledge and wisdom to only the few chosen for their special abilities including not falling asleep while he's talking, drinking out of damp glasses, or suffering from thrips.

4

Beer the Gardener

Amos Beer the great horticulturist began gardening at an early age when his parents made a second move 200 miles away while he was indisposed. He quickly dug himself out of the pit he had been accidentally knocked into and found he enjoyed not being buried in soil. A year or so later he was painting a fence a bright emerald green when someone said he had green fingers. This began his career as Head Gardener for a tribe of head hunters in the Amazon. He later worked for a tribe of pigmys, growing giant redwood bonzai trees to save cutting them down. When they gave up vegetarianism to become cannibals Beer moved back to England to join a long line of people at Queue Gardens, now called Kew, where his climbing roses escaped and he was unfairly dismissed. He then joined a local glee club and young pensioners group, that year winning the Britain in Gloom contest for flowers that had gone over.

Urged to work in central government and politics he said why should he if no-one else did, he'd rather play Russian Roulette with a fully loaded revolver and take his chances. Beer then founded the Royal Haughty Culture Society, writing several books on the garden until told he should have written them on paper he went on to university, obtaining The Three Degrees he'd always wanted and becoming their manager.

Film actresses called Ava named themselves after his gardener skills, then back in the Westcountry a village was named Westward Hoe in his honour as a man who called a spade a fork. Beer's leeks were so well known you could write your name in the snow with them, his cabbages and other greens becoming legendary to the extent an old friend Scouty called himself Broccoli, the name Scouty Broccoli now synonymous with spy films thanks to Beer.

But Beer had had enough of gardening. Still full of beans and still with a love of digging he turned to archaeology where menhirs were menhirs and womanhirs were womanhirs and all that stuff.

He put an old motor horn on his doorway in place of a door bell and instead of 'press' underneath it he wrote 'Toot'n come in', a phrase which would become famous throughout all Egypt soon after a fellow called Carter came to see him at his home. Carter was looking for advice, knowing Beer was already two or three days into his studies of Egyptian Archaeology.

"It's not a lot different than English archaeology", Beer told him, "just sandier in places. You must peer amid the sand dunes a bit more", peer amid being yet another phrase that would be linked to such excavations for all time thanks to Beer's expertise.

Carter was amazed. "But how shall I find something marvellous, I only have one more chance? he cried.

Beer gave him a handkerchief and waited for the man to compose himself.

"Compose yourself man. Act like a new piece of music" Beer told him. "Conduct yourself in the proper manner".

"Aye, I will", Carter said. Goodness now I'm stammering!"

"No. You said, Aye, I will, not I, I will" Beer told him.

"Thank goodness", Carter said.

"Now then Carter, what you must do is dig where the burial tombs of the great kings are, not where they are not, which is what you have been doing. I know you are a failure but give it one more try man", he said trying to cheer the man up as he was getting short of handkerchiefs.

"You are right as always" Carter exclaimed. "I shall go back to Egypt and take your advice".

"And I'll give you this little memento from beneath my hooter, there, 'Toot'n come in', put it over the door of the first tomb you find, just to remember me by."

Carter thanked him, asking if there were any further clues Beer could give him.

"Take this old chap", Beer said handing Carter a large sheet of brand new sandpaper. "See this cross I am making on it? That's where you will find what you are looking for. Right there in the sand".

"You're a genius", Carter told him.

"Oh, all right then", Beer said.

There are many other tales of Beer the archaeologist, many buried in the mists of time, but more of those later.

5

Beer the Astronaut

Kernel, sorry, Colonel Glen Beer, named after a Scottish valley where he used to spend his holidays. Yes, Beer was the old name for a Scottish valley, was the greatest of all astronauts.

It was his love for chocolate that drove him to follow this career. As a boy he would gaze at Mars, Galaxy, The Milky Way and Willie Wonka through his home made telescope and dream of reaching the stars. However his arms were far too short so he invented perpetual motion but he soon put a stop to that, deciding to make his fortune selling candles to aliens living on the dark side of the moon.

He then discovered weightlessness by jumping from cliffs and finding he was weightless all the way to the ground, and then, upon landing very heavily, realised he had invented craters similar to those on the moon, proving there was a genius like himself living on the moon.

Needing financial backing he sold hundreds of the craters he had made to people wanting ponds in their gardens, finding that each time he sold one and dug it up there was another larger one beneath. Now rich he decided to take a week off to build a spacecraft and by taking his time and with six days to spare he soon completed the task.

Sadly the first attempt fell back to Earth when only a few feet off the ground, Beer realising he had painted a 'Spaceship Made In England' logo on the side. He wandered disconsolately into the nearest cafe, grinned at the waitress and was suddenly struck by the idea of a flying saucer.

But, being a double genius and realising china clay would break on impact he made his UFO from an unknown metal shown to him by one of the aliens from Roswell who had shown US scientists how to make and programme microchips and modern computers.

Using an unknown metal, metal detector Beer soon found enough unknown metal to make a full tea set and dinner service but was told by the alien, "creen cardo vostle ruber nord klunk, heenin plonker dis orient ated" which is partly broken English for "all we need is a saucer. What more does an old crock like you need anyway," the alien said, his grasp of English very swift.

Beer's second attempt also failed but only because he had not waited for a full Moon and went through the dark bit. He sailed on into deep space, landing on Pluto, then Mickey Mouse and Goofy. On his return journey he ran rings around Saturn, couldn't find the Moon at all as it was then in eclipse, bounced off Neptune who was just finishing off a new invention Beer had sent him, a four pronged trident, and landed back on Earth.

Undismayed Beer sent out message after message into space using a very large jungle drum. After years of hoping he was eventually contacted and abducted by a craft filled with female aliens and after almost struggling he went with them to share his favourite hobbies, an act of kindness he could not resist.

As a true professional and loyal to his country he insisted on returning to Earth as soon as an intelligent Prime Minister and Government is found.

He was last heard shouting that famous phrase, "What's the chances of that happening eh?!"